Binding Ties

BINDING TIES

BY

C. S. ADLER

HAMISH HAMILTON LONDON

HAMISH HAMILTON CHILDREN'S BOOKS

Penguin Books Ltd, 27 Wrights Lane, London W8 5TZ (Publishing & Editorial)
and Harmondsworth, Middlesex, England (Distribution & Warehouse)
Viking Penguin inc., 40 West 23rd Street, New York, New York 10010, U.S.A.
Penguin Books Australia Ltd, Ringwood, Victoria, Australia
Penguin Books Canada Limited, 2801 John Street, Markham, Ontario, Canada L3R 1B4
Penguin Books (N.Z.) Ltd, 182-190 Wairau Road, Auckland 10, New Zealand

First published in Great Britain 1987 by
Hamish Hamilton Children's Books

First published in the USA 1985 by
Delacorte Press, New York

British Library Cataloguing-in-Publication Data:

Adler, C.S.
Binding ties.
I. Title
813'.54[F] PZ7

ISBN 0-241-12413-1

Printed and bound in Great Britain by
Butler and Tanner Ltd, Frome and London

1

Saturday morning. A whole weekend of hours ahead of her to spend with Kyle. Anne slid out of bed filled with joyous energy and dressed in clothes chosen to please him. Not her muted plaid shirt and chinos but a soft, gauzy blouse over snug-fitting pants. He liked sexy women and she tried to flute her prim edges for him. "My girl," he had called her last week. No compliment had ever thrilled her more.

She tiptoed past her sleeping mother, who had the hallside room of the partitioned attic. Sleeping late on weekends was a luxury for both her mother and her aunt Renee, the third occupant of the upper floor of Grams's house. The old stairs creaked under Anne's light step as she descended to Grams's domain. If only Grams were still asleep too! It would be refreshing to meet Kyle for once without having to endure the mosquito attack of Grams's disapproval. Anne rounded the curled end of the banister and came face-to-face with Renee, her sleek hair already combed, neat even in tailored housecoat and high-heeled scuffs.

"Up so soon?" Anne asked.

"Had to answer a call of nature. I'll be asleep again as soon as my head hits the pillow. What are you up for this early?"

"Kyle's picking me up at eight."

Renee's eyes focused on Anne's blouse. "*That's* what you're going to wear for him?"

"Yes."

"Can't say I admire your taste."

"He'll like it."

"That's what I'm afraid of. It's tacky, Anne. That's not the kind of girl you are."

"Oh, Renee, you worry too much about appearances. It's how people are inside that counts."

"No doubt, but others judge by what they see. He'll see a certain kind of invitation."

"Renee, leave me alone, please. I'm old enough to choose my own clothes. Besides, Mother was with me when I bought this blouse and she didn't object to it."

"Enjoy yourself, but not too much," Renee said sharply and slipped past Anne to head upstairs. Renee's feelings were hurt.

"Don't worry, I will," Anne said, and added to soothe her, "you have a good day too."

Renee stopped halfway up the stairs and blew a kiss. She never held a grudge the way Grams would. Anne smiled at her aunt and continued to the bathroom, which was too close to the kitchen and Grams's bedroom. As soon as Anne had turned off the water, Grams's voice pierced the closed bathroom door.

"Anne? Is that you? What are you up for?"

"Kyle's picking me up early today, Grams."

"You're not seeing him again! You were out with him last night. What about schoolwork?"

"Don't worry. They won't kick me off the honor roll." She

finished drying herself, tempted to hide out in the bathroom a while longer, but there was no way to avoid Grams now. Anne stepped into the kitchen.

Grams stood at the stove, favoring her bad hip and wielding a spatula. Surgical corset and stockings were already in place under her housedress and not a white hair escaped its tight setting. In her pinch-lipped face, only the thick eyebrows were untamed.

"I'm making you French toast," Grams said.

"I'd rather have cereal, thank you."

"You don't eat enough," Grams said and continued making the rich egg-and-sugar-soaked toast.

"Well, just one piece, then, please," Anne said. No answer. Grams would serve her two. She ruled the kitchen, as she tried to rule the rest of their lives, in the certainty that she knew what was best for them. Only Renee escaped total domination because Grams respected her oldest daughter's ability in the business world. Renee had, as Grams put it, "made a success of herself." Lily, Anne's mother, hadn't made a success of anything.

"Why your mother lets you see so much of that boy is beyond me," Grams continued as she slapped the toast on a plate and set it down on the table in front of Anne. "No good will come of it, believe you me."

"Kyle's a nice boy, Grams. I don't know why you have it in for him."

"Nice boy! Nice boys have manners. Nice boys don't drive like maniacs."

"How would you know how he drives when you've never been in a car with him, Grams?" Anne took a bite of the toast and tried to swallow it.

"I hear him come into the driveway like he's going to drive

right through the house," Grams said. "Then he bangs on the horn for you instead of coming to the door like a gentleman."

Anne thought of Kyle's advice. "Don't let her get your goat. Change the subject and laugh it off." Kyle was an expert on confrontation. His father was always on his back about something. Anne tried. "This toast is delicious, Grams. Thanks for making it for me."

Grams sniffed. "It's the way I always make it." She returned to the attack. "Even your mother says you spend too much time with him. Would it hurt you to stay home with your family once in a while?"

"I'm sixteen. It's normal for a sixteen-year-old girl to spend a lot of time with her boyfriend."

"Normal for young girls to get in trouble, too," Grams said.

"I'm not going to get in trouble," Anne yelled suddenly. "Why do you accuse me of things I've never done? Haven't I always been a good girl?"

"Don't you raise your voice to me," Grams said. "That's his influence. Your family doesn't mean a thing to you anymore."

"Grams, please!" Anne pleaded. "Kyle is my first real boyfriend. Can't you let me enjoy my life a little?"

"And what about your mother? Doesn't she deserve to enjoy too? After all she's been through, it shouldn't be too much for you to spend some time with her."

It was impossible to win, Anne thought, useless to point out that she was home almost every school night.

"She spoiled you," Grams said. "She could never say no to you. I told her she'd regret it. You don't care about anyone but yourself now."

Impulsively, Anne tossed the French toast on her plate into the garbage. Trembling with frustration, she said, "Why must you make me feel guilty when I haven't done anything wrong?"

"You're all your mother has left," Grams said. Her tearful look always brought Renee and Lily to their knees, but Anne withstood it.

"She has you and Renee," Anne said.

"You're the one she lives for."

Anne squeezed her eyes shut. It was true. Lily had suffered like Job—divorce and cancer and the loss of Anne's little brother, Chip. Lily did need her and Anne did love her mother very much, but Kyle had taught her happiness and she craved being with him. "I'll be home by three anyway. Mother's taking me shopping."

"And who for? Not for her sake I'm sure."

Anne clamped her lips shut and began to rinse her plate in the sink.

"Use soap," Grams said. "Where's he taking you today?"

"I don't know."

"You're not leaving without telling us where you're going?"

"I'll ask Kyle when he gets here, but he doesn't always plan in advance."

"And you'll stay home with us tonight?"

"Grams, can't you *ever* stop nagging me?"

Grams's eyes turned tragic. "The way you talk to me," she cried. "When you were a little girl, you'd sit in my lap and say you loved me. All I want is to see you grow up right. Is that so terrible?"

Anne knew her duty and with a sigh she did it. "I still love you," she said and forced herself to kiss her grandmother's cheek. Then resentment made her add, "If only you wouldn't pick on me all the time."

"I don't pick. I watch out for you. You know you're all we have left since we lost Chip."

Anne suffered the flash of grief still familiar a year after her little brother's death. Usually they avoided mentioning his name to protect each other, but Grams cared too much about winning to mind the unwritten rule.

Grams sniffed. "Maybe once your stepsister gets here next week, you'll stay home more."

Anne snatched at the change of subject. "It'll be fun to have Dodie around, won't it?"

Grams nodded. She approved of Dodie, who enjoyed gabbing with the family for hours at a time. When Anne glanced at the clock over the sink, Grams said, "I just hope he doesn't blast that horn and wake your mother."

"I'll wait for him outside."

It was a relief to escape into the cool September morning even though Anne knew it wasn't over yet. Grams would complain to Lily, who would dutifully dab on a little criticism tonight about the way Anne had spoken to Grams. "Your grandmother has had a hard life," Mother always pointed out, but it seemed to Anne a poor excuse for making everybody else's life hard too. She had liked her grandmother better at a distance, before Lily's illness had made it necessary for them all to live together. "She means well," Lily would also say, but that didn't alleviate the nagging.

Grams's front yard was overgrown with trees, more moss and bare dirt than patches of grass. The concrete walk to the driveway had heaved and cracked. The house needed painting. Grams had lived here on the same city street for forty years, twenty since her husband had died and left her the house and an insurance policy too small to support her. Neighbors had come and gone. Now the old houses were populated with young couples who kept to themselves. Renee talked about having some trees cut down and the brown trim on the Tudor-style house freshly painted, but Grams didn't really care what her house looked like. Neither did Anne. Where she lived now didn't matter. School didn't matter. Nothing mattered but Kyle. Grams was right about that.

Of course, he was late again. He thought nothing of turning morning dates into afternoon. Not that it was his fault. It happened because his father would assign him some unexpected task, or his car would break down, or a friend would need him in an emergency.

"If you'd only call and tell me you're going to be late," she had begged once.

"Don't nag," he told her. "Don't you ever try and change me." And his jaw had set and the look in his eyes had warned her, even though the finger touching her cheek was tender. If he came late, she consoled herself by thinking it was a miracle that he came at all. She was pretty, but so many of the girls who buzzed around him were prettier. And her prettiness was somber. She had light brown hair and brown eyes, pale skin that never tanned and seemed too thin over the delicate bones of her oval face and tall, slender body. A sadness shadowed her lips and eyes. "Such a serious girl," Kyle had said just before he kissed her the first time.

She wondered if he would make time for them to be alone today. Sometimes he didn't, as if his need was not as urgent as hers. For her the best time was when it was just the two of them in private, where his hands and lips could find her and the complications of their lives disappeared. She had been surprised to discover what a hunger she had for physical love. Grams would be horrified if she knew.

And what would her stepsister, Dodie, think? Though Anne had written her so much about Kyle, she had never mentioned sex. Too private. But when Dodie was here, then what? Anne bit her lower lip. To have her one and only sister-friend living with her from September through Christmas should be the most incredible treat, but she hadn't told Kyle about it yet. Foolish to worry about his reaction. He liked people, all kinds of people, and Dodie was fun. She'd tell him today, the minute he arrived.

2

As usual he came roaring down the hill. He did everything top speed. It was part of his attraction that the world moved faster when she was with him. Anne opened the door and called into the house, "Kyle's here and I'm leaving."

"Where's he taking you?" Grams asked from the door of the kitchen.

"I'll call if I can. I'll be back by three." She ran before Grams could protest.

"Hey, you're all dressed up," he said as she slid into the car seat next to him. No excuses even though he was an hour late. She smiled at him as he fingered the blouse. "Pretty," he said. "Everything about you is pretty and you smell good too."

He stopped the car at the corner out of sight of the house and embraced her. "I like your scent better," she said. He smelled of leather and oil and sweat.

He laughed. Then he kissed her and the suffocating atmosphere of Grams's house blew away, leaving only the freshness of the morning they had to share.

"Kyle," she said quickly. "Guess what? I'm going to have a houseguest next week. Dodie's coming."

"For how long?"

"Until Christmas."

"Four months? You're not serious."

Anne explained that Dodie's mother was giving seminars out west and that Larry, Anne's father and Dodie's stepfather, was taking time off from his real estate business to go along.

"Dodie's temporarily orphaned."

"Is she still fat?" Kyle asked.

"What does that matter?"

"Because if she's a baby elephant, how're we going to unload her on anybody?"

"Dodie makes friends as easily as you do," Anne said. "She has a wonderful personality."

"Boyfriends?"

"Oh, Kyle!"

"Well, face it, baby. She may be your best friend—"

"And my sister."

"And your father may be married to her mother, making her your stepsister, not your sister—"

"And when Chip was killed, she came and stood by me all through the funeral."

"And she may be a good kid and fun to be with and all that, but she's still gonna get in our way. Three's a crowd."

"Well, I can't help it."

"Okay," he said. "Don't look so desperate. We'll handle it." He cushioned her head in his hand and kissed her again in that sure way that made her melt.

"Where are we off to today?" she asked.

"First to see a guy about some car parts he promised me. Then somebody's offered me in on a deal that I gotta check out. You don't mind a little ride in the country, do you?"

"Not so long as I'm with you."

She clung to the door going around corners and braced herself at stops, enjoying equal parts of the grin on his face and the passage of sunshot fields, barns billowing up red, light reflected off the shiny domes of silos.

"Doesn't she respond great now that I've got her tuned up right?" he asked.

"Great." She didn't know a thing about cars.

"Brakes are wearing out, though."

She laughed. "You're always wearing out brakes."

He gave her a quick glance. "Yeah, I know. Next I'm going to take flying lessons. It'd be awesome to wing through the sky with no old ladies in the lane ahead of me." He angled by the left rear fender of one such slow-moving driver, out into the opposing lane of traffic and back in. Anne glanced back at the shocked face of the gray-haired woman in the car and sank low in the seat in embarrassment.

"You're terrible," she said.

"I know it. How come you put up with me?"

"Nobody's perfect."

"You are, Anne."

"That's not a compliment. Perfect is boring. So is being mature for your age, which is what everybody always says I am."

"You're fine," he said. "Just around adults too much. You need to learn how to play. That's why I'm so good for you."

"Yes," she said. It was true. He was good for her. Despite what her family thought, he was very good.

He had been a lifeguard the summer Anne met him. At just seventeen, he was the youngest lifeguard they had ever hired at the town pool, but he seemed much older. The girls fluttered around him and he flirted with them, grinning, teasing, a big, handsome guy, friendly to everyone. All except Anne. She sat in the shade with her ever-present book in hand, keeping an eye on her little brother. She only went into the pool to get wet when the sun got too hot. At fifteen, wrapped tight inside herself, she'd had nothing to do all summer but take Chip to the pool and try to teach herself Latin, a self-imposed task. Chip spent his time in the water, under the water mostly. The first positive notice Anne took of Kyle Youngman was because he was so nice to her little brother. "How ya doing, Chip?" Kyle would say and Chip would swell with pride at being singled out. Kyle gave Chip pointers on swimming techniques along with plenty of encouragement.

"I'm going to be a lifeguard like Kyle when I grow up," Chip would say.

Anne had to admit that Kyle was a good-humored guy. When kids played tricks on him—hid his whistle, tried to swipe his towel—he took the teasing gracefully. His authority impressed her too. He could discipline the rowdies, make them stop roughhousing in the water or running on slippery surfaces or shoving other kids into the pool. "You!" he'd say, pointing. "Cut that out." They'd quit, and Anne would shiver with satisfaction. Although he never noticed her, she'd admitted him into her daydreams. She liked the strength in his rugged face, imagined depths below the easygoing surface. But his taste in women ran to small, voluptuous females who paraded on his arm after hours or on his breaks.

It made Anne's heart pound to see him slide a casual hand down a girl's back and watch her lean her breasts against his long, muscular body. Anne not only wasn't his type, she wouldn't really know what to do about it if she were. His sexuality scared her everywhere but in her dreams.

The summer ended. Anne began her sophomore year. Kyle

was a junior. Still he gave no sign he recognized her from the summer at the pool—not until after Chip was killed on his bicycle at the intersection of Balltown Road and Nott Street.

She returned to school a week later, still in a state of shock, and Kyle greeted her in the hall. "Hey, I heard about your little brother. I'm really sorry. He was a neat kid."

She began to cry, great heaving sobs that had been stuck inside her and that hurt coming out. She couldn't help it. "Hey," he said, "hey, I'm sorry. I didn't mean to set you off." He put his arm around her and hugged her, then searched his pockets for a handkerchief, not finding any. She dug some tissues from her canvas purse.

"Skip your class," he said. "Let's go to the cafeteria and have a Coke or something." Numbly she went with him. To her embarrassment she heard herself telling him all about it in detail—the ride to the hospital, the sight of Chip wrapped in bandages with only his eyes and mouth showing, the endless night so swiftly over when Chip died, the things she'd meant to get him and do with him and never did, his sweetness, his love for animals, and how unfair it was.

"I lost a brother too," Kyle said, somewhere in all that. "My older brother. He was the best of us. He got it in a motorcycle accident." Then he told her about his eleven-year-old twin brothers. "See, they have each other, the way my older brother and I had each other. Without him I stick out like a sore thumb in our family. I'm the one my father wishes he didn't have." They talked for hours. She had never cut a class in her life, but she had no regrets about that afternoon.

The first time Grams met Kyle, she'd said, "You mark my words. That boy is trouble," and she'd tried to make Lily forbid Anne to go out with Kyle. Usually Lily did what Grams wanted, but this time Lily had said that Anne was mature enough to make her own judgments.

"I don't think he's Anne's type," Renee had put in even though no one asked her.

"I like him," Anne had said simply, knowing the type Renee expected for her, a future college professor or business executive, all buttoned up and boring.

"I know I can trust you," Lily said to her privately.

Anne was proud of her mother's trust. She'd had no idea then of breaking it.

"This guy we're going to drop in on is a little flaky," Kyle said. "Lives in a trailer with a woman and her three little kids. She's gotta be twice his age."

"Does he go to school?"

"Just got out of jail." He turned his wolfish grin full on her, his eyes teasing. "Your grandmother would have a heart attack if she knew what ba-a-a-a-ad company you're keeping."

"I'm with you and you're not bad."

"That so? My dad thinks I'm the worst."

"You have another go-around this morning?"

"Well, sure. How else would I start the day?"

"What was it about this time?"

"Seems I left the shower head turned to 'on' so he got a blast of cold water. After he laid me out over that one, he found oil on his garage floor and nailed me for fixing my car there again. Did you know the garage is not the place for cars? At least not clunkers like mine that leak oil. But the worst was —now get this—one of my good buddies woke him up by calling at eleven last night. That was really my fault, wasn't it?"

"I guess you're bad all right."

"Yeah, every family has a black sheep and I'm ours."

"Someday," she assured him, "you'll make your father proud of you."

"Think so, baby?" He looked hopeful. "I'd like to. I'd like to hit him in the eye from the front page of *The Wall Street Journal.* 'Dynamic young innovator of blah blah blah comes out tops in the industry's survey for getting there fastest with the mostest.' He wanted my brother to be a Harvard Business School graduate someday. All he expects from me is to stay out of jail."

Handsome, she thought, even if his nose was too bulky. His eyes were expressive, and he radiated energy. She leaned against his shoulder until they jounced over the railroad crossing, then pounded down a dirt road to a hillside blistered with cars and abandoned refrigerators and children's rusting bicycles. Three kids sat in front of a white trailer, combing the burrs from a big shaggy dog.

"How's it going?" Kyle greeted the wasted-looking fellow who climbed down from the truck body on which he was working.

"Doing okay, Kyle. How're you?" They shook hands. Anne watched them talking, fascinated as always at how Kyle could relate to all kinds of people. If only she could exude such warmth.

"How about a couple of beers?" the skinny fellow asked, including Anne in a sliding glance that ended up back on Kyle.

"No, thanks, ole buddy." It was midmorning. "We've got to get moving. Did you find those parts you said you had?"

"Sure, got them all picked out back here." He gestured at the hill behind the trailer and said to Anne, "Maybe you want to visit with Betty awhile? She's inside getting breakfast."

Anne was startled. "Oh, that's okay," she said. "I'll just wait here." No way would she knock on the door and introduce herself to a stranger. Kyle hadn't even introduced her to his friend. She felt awkward, the way she felt at parties when Kyle left her stranded and got involved with someone. Her own fault for being so shy. She sat down on the cinder block step at the door of the trailer and watched the children struggle with the matted coat of the big wag-tailed dog.

"He's supposed to stay tied up, but he got away," the middle-sized child said.

"He seems to like all the attention you're giving him," Anne answered.

"He gets away again, Mama's gonna beat him," the smallest child offered.

It seemed to take a long time for Kyle to finish his business. Anne stirred restlessly. She'd learned to tolerate his habit of cramming all sorts of activities having nothing to do with her into a weekend, but she didn't have to like it. He returned finally, carrying an armload of metal parts that he piled in the trunk of the car.

"So what do I owe you, Martin?" he said to the skinny guy.

"Nothing. Forget it. You done me a favor. I can do something for you."

"No, I want to pay you. One thing's got nothing to do with the other."

They argued back and forth, repeating themselves. Kyle won and money changed hands. Martin looked happy pocketing the cash. They shook and Martin nodded once at Anne, who got into the car and smiled good-bye at him, waving at the children.

"Poor guy," Kyle said. "He just lost his job at the warehouse. Got caught drinking on the premises. Bad news."

"What favor did you do for him?"

"Oh, nothing much. Told the police he was with me when

he wasn't. He's got enough trouble without getting pulled in for questioning again. Hungry?"

"A little." It was past noon.

"This guy who has the deal I need to check out owns a lakeside bar. It's closed for the season, but maybe he'll cook up something for us."

"If not we can go to my house and I'll make you a cheese omelet. I learned how because you said you liked them."

"And face the dragon lady? No way. Not today. One person beating on me is enough. I have to answer any of your grandma's loaded questions and I'll be down for the count. This guy's got a speedboat anyway. It's kind of fun on a nice warm day like today."

"Sure." Meeting strangers was hard for her, but that was what being with Kyle usually meant. Like any bad-tasting medicine, it was probably good for her. She took a deep breath and let it out slowly.

"I left you sitting there for too long at the trailer, huh?" he said.

"That's okay."

"Don't worry. This time we'll stick together."

"You read me too well."

"How come you're so pretty?" He drew her in close. "You look so cool, and your skin's like silk." One finger caressed her cheek. It was enough to make her happy.

The Lake Inn was a shabby wooden house with a bar and a few tables. The manager was stout with hooded eyes.

"How's it going, Emmet?" Kyle asked him.

"Lousy." The manager looked Anne up and down as if she were a side of beef. "Changed your style in women, Kyle?"

"Sort of."

"You're going for class now. I'm impressed."

He was talking to Kyle. Anne wasn't sure whether to be

complimented or insulted at being treated like an object. When Kyle asked about lunch, Emmet said he hadn't gotten to the market.

"You ready to discuss the deal or not?" he asked Kyle.

"I'm ready."

"Sit down, then. Your girl can check out the speedboat down by the dock while we're talking."

Kyle shrugged apologetically at Anne, who set off obediently for the water's edge to daydream the time away.

"What's the matter with him?" she asked when Kyle joined her in the speedboat an hour later.

"You probably remind him of his wife. She was the cool, elegant type too. She just left him."

"Oh . . . Was the deal any good?"

"Too good. I told him I had to think about it. He's mad, but he said we could use the boat anyway."

Eagerly, Kyle untied the lines that secured the boat to the dock, then got behind the wheel. Speed! If she had a V-8 engine in her, he'd adore her, Anne thought. She sat back against the vinyl cushions. She would have been scared with anyone but Kyle, who was ripping through the water as if he were trying to tear the lake apart. The noise was tremendous and the jolting hard to get used to as they circled back on their own wake. Kyle stood, yelling exuberantly. Anne caught only the echo of his excitement. Finally he stopped, shut the engine down to idle, and asked, "Like it?"

"Now I do," she said.

"Scared?"

"Not with you. Why do you enjoy it so much?"

"I don't know. I like to move fast. That's why school gets to me. I can shoot the bull okay, but I hate sitting there while some teacher talks at me."

"But you'll go to college anyway, won't you?"

"Would you love me even if I don't, Anne?"

"I might."

She offered him her lips, and for a while they kissed in the sunshine, rocked by the boat on the gently slapping water. Eventually he revved up the engine and sped them back to shore.

"Call me on it soon," Emmet told Kyle when they left. "Nice meeting you," he said to Anne, his eyes assessing her again in that calculating way.

"Are you going to tell me about the deal?" she asked Kyle.

"He's got sports equipment he wants me to sell in the high school—expensive stuff. I buy it from him cheap and keep whatever profit I make on the sale. I could make plenty, but I'm sure the goods are hot. Somebody robbed a warehouse somewhere."

"You're not going to do it?"

"No, too risky."

"You don't need money all that much, do you?" She knew his car kept him short of cash, but he always seemed to find a fill-in job when he needed extra money.

"Listen, Anne," he said. "The only way to make it big in this world is to get rich or get professional degrees. If I can't sit still for school, I'd better scratch up some seed money soon so I have a shot at getting rich."

"Okay," she said. "We'll start economizing by eating lunch at my house. If you don't want an omelet, I could make you a peanut butter and jelly sandwich."

"You got quince jam?"

She mimicked his bad speech. "No, I don't got quince jam."

"No good, then. I got to have quince jam with my peanut butter. We'll have a pizza instead, huh?"

"I thought we were going to save money."

"Dollars, not pennies."

He played with her fingers on the red checked tablecloth as they waited for their pizza to be baked. "Tell me about the twins," she said, thinking of the oldest boy at the trailer and how he had reminded her of Chip.

"They're still winning swim meets and bringing home A's," he said. "They make up for me."

"You could bring home A's if you wanted. You could win sports events too."

"Yeah. My older brother did that. He was so smart. The twins got to crack the books, but he didn't."

"Weren't you ever jealous of him, Kyle?"

"Couldn't be. It just came so naturally to him. Besides, he liked me. I used to make him laugh. Did you know I'm the family clown as well as resident bad boy?"

"You aren't either. You're a serious person."

"I don't know what I am, Anne. I'm pretty sure what you are, but damned if I know what I am."

"And what am I?"

"You're my girl. You're Kyle's old lady." He touched a finger to her lips. She bit the finger lightly.

"Here's your pizza," the unsmiling waitress said, setting it down between them.

"Ummm. I could eat the whole thing. You don't want any, Annie, do you?"

"Only four or five pieces."

"Glutton. Look how little of you there is to fill." They shared the last piece bite by bite between them. The waitress wasn't amused. Kyle left a big tip anyway.

In the car he kissed her hard. "Sometimes you are just so lovable," he said.

She glowed. Only he had ever called her lovable.

"Want to go somewhere and neck?" he whispered into the hollow at the base of her neck.

The ready desire slithered through her. "Yes," she breathed, and then remembered. "But we don't have long. I have to be back home by three."

"It's past that now."

"Oh, no! Kyle!"

Without another word he drove her home. "Tonight," he said as she got out of the car at the foot of her driveway.

"Tonight," she promised.

3

"How could you do that to your mother?" Grams asked, cutting short Anne's rush of apologies. "She's been waiting for you all afternoon."

"Mom, I'm so sorry. I had no idea how late it was. I just completely lost track of the time."

"Well, the Clothes Gallery is closed now," Lily said, putting down her coffee cup and trying to cover her obvious disappointment with a smile. "Maybe the sale will still be on next week. You do need a new dress, Anne."

"That old paisley she wears for good looks so shabby," Renee commented. "You know, the stores in the mall are open tonight. We could go after dinner."

"Afraid not," Anne said. "Kyle said something about a movie. It *is* Saturday night."

"You spent last night and all day today with him," Renee pointed out.

"I don't think the mall is such a good idea," Grams said.

"You're not going to find anything on sale there, Lily. You'll overspend again."

"We could look, Mama. How about inviting Kyle to come with us to the mall?" Lily said to Anne.

"I don't think he'd want to—I mean, shopping for clothes for me?" Anne grimaced, imagining Kyle's impatience.

"If Anne can't be bothered going, let her do without then," Grams said. "All she wants is to be with that boy."

"Grams, I said I was sorry."

"Saying is one thing. Showing is another. Never mind. No one cares what I think in this family anyway." Grams banged pots around on the stove. Lily and Renee exchanged glances. Then Lily began reassuring Grams of her importance while Renee toyed with one of the large gold rings she wore. Her long, polished fingernails clicked against the metal. Renee's eyes were made up, her lipstick perfectly applied. That meant she'd gone somewhere today, probably to her office to finish answering the week's backlog of mail. She often did that on Saturdays.

"You do seem to be seeing a lot of Kyle lately," Renee said. "You don't want to give him the idea you're at his beck and call, do you?"

"Why not, Renee? I don't play games with Kyle."

"It's not smart to let a man take you for granted," Renee said.

How do you know? Anne wanted to say. There were no men in Renee's life as far as Anne knew, but she held her tongue and asked instead, "Aren't we going to eat soon? I'm sorry I didn't get here in time to set the table." It was hopeless. She could never be sorry enough.

"And you're going to leave before doing the dishes again," Grams said.

"Oh, leave her alone, Mama," Renee said. "Look, Anne, it

wouldn't hurt you to spend an evening with your family once in a while."

"Let's not make such a big thing of this," Lily said.

"I'll call Kyle and tell him I'll see him tomorrow." They looked at her, the guilty one. She smiled. "Okay?"

Lily smiled back, her doughy face soft with love. "That would be nice, darling."

As she stood in the narrow hall at the drop leaf table dialing Kyle's number, Anne could hear them rehashing their positions. They were analyzing the exact degree of her involvement with Kyle Youngman. They were always analyzing. Anne was tired of it.

"Just because we were a little late?" Kyle asked when she told him she couldn't see him tonight.

"Just because I owe it to my mother."

"What about what you owe me?"

"Oh, Kyle, we'll see each other tomorrow. Please, don't be angry with me. I can't stand another person being angry with me tonight."

"They come first. Okay. If that's how it is. I'll call you." He hung up. She stood miserably beside the phone table.

"Dinner's ready, Anne," Lily said, entering the dark hall. Then, coming closer, she put her arms around her daughter. "Something wrong, darling?"

"No, Mom. I'm all right."

"Are you seeing him tomorrow?"

"I don't know."

"Did he give you a hard time?"

"It's all right, Mom."

"He was angry at you? . . . Well, honey, really—one disappointment shouldn't wreck your relationship if it's worth anything at all, right?"

"I hope so." Anne took a deep breath and stood up straighter.

"That's my sensible girl. Come and have your dinner."

Anne had always been close to her mother. Before the bad times, when Lily was still married to Larry, Lily had been a giddy, soft, talkative young mother who seemed to be playing house. She would laugh at all the messes she and Anne made trying out new recipes in the kitchen. She would giggle about spending too much money on clothes and furnishings. She would consult Anne about bringing up Chip or when she had secrets like overdrawn checking accounts to hide from Larry.

In those days Grams would come for an annual two-week visit and divide her time between criticizing Larry for not making enough money and educating Lily on how to run a household and raise children. Grams had approved of Anne then, bestowing the highest praise on her when she said, "You're just like your Aunt Renee." Grams boasted often, "Renee makes a better income than a lot of men," and was convinced the only reason Renee hadn't married was she hadn't found a man good enough for her. Anne had always been relieved when Grams went home.

Then in quick succession came the divorce and Mother's failures—trying to start an antiques business, trying to find another husband. When the lump in her breast turned out to be cancer and Lily really needed her family's support after her mastectomy, they moved in with Grams and Renee. And Anne had had to watch Lily slip back into a childlike dependence on her mother and sister.

"Disasters come in threes," Grams had said when Chip was killed on his bicycle. Of them all, Grams survived that loss best. Anne still ached when anything reminded her of him and when she awoke from dreams of him and realized he was dead. Renee had been the most hysterical, unlike herself for days. Lily had been totally deboned. Now she seemed content to float along without thought of any future. She worked in the dress shop, a job Grams had gotten for her. She was still sweet and loving, still optimistic for Anne if not for herself. Her comfort came from eating, and her prettiness was lost in the lines of pain and in marshmallow fat. Still, Anne loved her mother more than she pitied her. To spend time with her was not a duty but a pleasure. Normally. If there weren't the more urgent pull of Kyle.

"Renee's going shopping with us," Lily announced. "Isn't that nice?"

Anne looked at her mother. Renee's taste ran to expensive clothes that suited a career woman, not a teen-age girl—and Renee, like Grams, never doubted her own taste. But Anne recognized the message in her mother's tone of voice. Include Renee, poor Renee who'd never had a husband or a child of her own to share with. "Nice," Anne agreed reluctantly. Sympathy had a high price in their family.

"Why don't you come too, Mama?" Renee urged over the canned peaches Grams served for dessert. "We haven't all gone shopping together for ages."

"I'd just hold you back," Grams said. "You three go ahead and have a good time."

Usually the hint of martyrdom would bring assurances that she was wanted, but tonight Lily said only, "Grams has her Saturday-night shows to watch. She wouldn't like to miss them."

Renee's angular face was animated by the thought of clothes. "You must be a size eight like me," she said to Anne. Renee was proud that her size never changed. Grams often said, "Renee's got the figure and Lily's got the face." Renee joked about her "boyfriends"—the newsstand admirer, the actor in her dreams, the ideal male she'd meet someday—but

Anne had never seen evidence of any real men being interested in Renee.

"I wish *I* were a size eight again," Lily said as she put cream in her coffee.

"You look fine," Grams said. "A little weight looks good on you."

"Not really, Mama. I've gotten too fat, but who cares? The customers don't want me looking better in clothes than they do, and you all love me fat or thin."

"It's not healthy to carry too much extra weight," Renee said carefully.

"You've always had a thing about weight, Renee. You always cared more than I did."

That was the tip of an old iceberg. Out of Mother's hearing, Anne had once heard Grams tell Renee, "Leave your sister alone. What pleasure does she have now besides eating?"

"She could still find a man if she took better care of herself," Renee had said.

But Grams had answered, "What does she need with another husband? What did the first one bring her but trouble? She's best off with us."

As Anne expected, it was Renee who chose the store and who selected the dresses for Anne. "They're either too expensive or they make me look forty-two," Anne whispered to her mother when Renee bustled from the fitting room to find more.

"You look so lovely in everything," Lily said. "Find what you like, but don't say anything. Renee has very good taste."

"Not for me."

"Here you go, darling." Renee swept into the dressing room with an armload of dresses, crowding the place so that

Anne could barely see herself in the mirror. They finally settled on a simple blue dress that Anne thought Kyle would like.

"Didn't we have fun tonight?" Renee said, and insisted on treating them to ice-cream sundaes. They brought one home in a pint-size container for Grams.

That night Anne was hanging her new dress in her closet when Lily slopped into the bedroom in her scuffs and loose robe. She sat down on Anne's bed and said, "It *was* a nice evening, wasn't it? I'm so glad we included Renee. She loves you so, Anne."

"I love her, too, but not as a shopping companion."

"Well, it worked out all right, didn't it? I only wish I could afford to buy you more. You're such a beautiful girl, and so good besides."

"I'm not as good as you think, Mom."

"You're not?" Lily smiled indulgently. "How are you bad?"

Anne was thinking of her appetite for lovemaking. Lily wasn't so old-fashioned as to consider Anne a bad girl because of it, but it would certainly worry Lily, and Anne didn't want her mother to worry. Better say nothing. Briefly, Anne wondered if Larry would like Kyle any better than Grams and Renee did. Larry was liberal and easygoing, but he'd probably be anxious about this too. It made no difference anyway. Her father was too far away to count. She'd even learned not to miss him much.

Sunday morning Kyle did call, but not until Anne had spent hours worrying that he might not. "I'll pick you up at two," he said.

The sound of his voice made her bold. "Kyle, will you come in and say hello this time?"

"Do I have to?"

"I want them to know you. Please!"

"Three against one. They'll eat me alive."

She had thought he might come in anyway, but when he arrived, at two ten, he only stood in the doorway of the living room and said to the company at large, "We have to get going. Gonna be late. Sorry I can't stay. You ladies have a nice afternoon." And in answer to the inevitable question: "No, I won't keep her out too late."

"I've got us a place," he exulted when they were alone in the car. Then he drove madly to a tiny lake she'd never heard of. A friend had given him a key to a small one-room bungalow. Kids were always giving Kyle things, doing him favors to win his favor.

The rag rug on the floor in front of the couch was none too clean, but his body, hard on top of hers, made her forget that. It never ceased to amaze her at how violently her body responded to his. All he had to do was touch her with his eyes to set off a longing in her. Even the ugliness of the contraceptive he wore didn't faze her. She was hooked on the surge of hot blood racing through her, on the tingling in her loins and breasts. She loved the tickling feel of his body hair against her skin, and the way his hands cupping her breasts or buttocks or head made those parts of her feel beautiful. His breath and his nibbling, sucking mouth teased ecstasy from her. She wanted more of him, all of him. Nothing she had ever known had thrilled her as much as making love with Kyle Youngman.

"I wish we always had a place like this to come to," she said when they were resting, nestled together on the rug.

"It would be nice, but after next Sunday Baker's folks will be back to use it."

"Next Sunday Dodie's coming. I'll have to spend the day with her."

"What do you mean? You're not going to see me?"

"Kyle, I told you how much she means to me."

"Who means more?"

"You do."

"Then let your folks take care of her Sunday. She's going to be with you for months."

"I can't do that to her."

He sat up frowning, scaring her with the ominous narrowing of his eyes. "Listen, baby, I'm working Saturday. Forget the whole weekend if you can't make it Sunday."

"Kyle!" She sat up and reached for her shirt to cover her nakedness. "Don't be unreasonable, please. You know I'd rather be with you than anybody."

"I come in second or third everywhere else in my life, Anne. With my girl it's gotta be first or forget it."

She stared at him, speechless. How could he sit there and make demands like that? "We're not married," she said.

"You liked it when those kids pointed you out as 'Kyle's girl,' didn't you? What'd you think they meant? Just that I go out with you? I go out with lots of girls. I've had lots of girls. You're the first one I've ever wanted to make mine."

She shivered with pleasure. She had been lonely for so long. "Oh, Kyle," she gasped, and threw herself at him. "I love you most and best and always. I love you."

"Hey," he said. "Hey, let's not get all charged up about it. Come on, come on." He kissed her and they cuddled each other until it was time to go.

"I'm Kyle's girl, Kyle's old lady. I'm Kyle's girl, Kyle's old lady" went the joyful singing in her head as she ran from his car to her house. She turned to wave when he tooted a good-bye. "Kyle's girl, Kyle's old lady." She unlocked the front door and found Renee on her knees beside Grams, who was crumpled in her chair, weeping.

"What's happened?" Anne cried, immediately thinking of her mother.

"Nothing, Anne. Nothing's wrong. Grams is worked up because your mother's been napping all afternoon."

"She's always tired. That's a sign, isn't it?" Grams said, referring to the cancer and the possibility that it could come back.

"She stands on her feet every day at the shop and that's tiring, Mama," Renee said. "The doctor says she's okay. Don't worry." Renee kept patting Grams's arm in a weary rhythm.

"I'll go up and see how she is," Anne said, and ran upstairs.

Lily was asleep on her bed, covered by the rose and wine afghan Grams had knitted for her. Anne listened to her mother's quiet breathing and wondered. Were they keeping secrets again, Renee and Mother—protecting Grams, protecting her from the awful truths of death and disease and disaster? If she woke her mother and asked her, Lily would smile and say she was fine. She had done that right up to the day she went into the hospital. Anne had been so angry at not being told then that she'd made both Renee and Lily swear they would not leave her out of any secrets ever again.

Back downstairs, Anne said, "She's all right, Grams. She probably stayed up too late reading last night. You know the way she is when she wants to finish a book."

"She looked all right to you?"

"She looks fine. Remember how pale she used to get? Her color's good now. She's healthy, Grams, really."

"Oh, God, I hope so! The trouble she's had since your father left her—and she was such a happy girl before!"

"It certainly wasn't my father's fault."

"Whose was it, then?"

Anne looked at Renee, who shrugged and said, "How about going for a walk with your old aunt? I need some fresh air."

"All right, Renee."

"Don't stay out too long," Grams said. "It's almost time for supper."

"We'll be back soon." Renee exchanged a look with Grams that Anne recognized from long experience. The family had had a conference and Renee had been delegated to speak to Anne about something. What now?

"*Is* something wrong with Mother?" Anne asked when they were a safe distance from the house.

"Not that I know of. The doctor says she's doing fine."

"Then what did you want to talk to me about?"

"Can't I just want to be alone with you for a change?" Renee smiled. "We used to go for lots of walks together, you and I. We were pals—B.K., before Kyle."

"I always enjoy your company, Renee, when we do things together—just as pals."

"Look, I know Grams irritates you, and I certainly don't want to nag you too, but I do want to talk to you." Renee took a deep breath and plunged in. "This Kyle Youngman is monopolizing your whole life, and to be honest, I find it hard to see what he has for you."

"Just himself."

"Don't be flip. What do you see in him?"

"He's a wonderful person," Anne said.

"He's older than you are and a whole lot more experienced. I suppose that blinds you to his defects."

Anne stiffened. "You don't know him at all. You all tell me I'm mature, but Mother is the only one who really trusts my judgment."

"Anne, you know I adore you. You're the child I never had. If I weren't worried, I wouldn't dream of interfering."

"What's he ever done to make you dislike him so much?"

"It's not what he's done," Renee said. "It's what he is—irresponsible and sloppy, the kind of fellow who uses girls. He'll take advantage of you, Annie."

"He won't. Just because he dresses casually, that's why you call him sloppy. As for irresponsible, I don't know what you mean by that," Anne said.

"Well, I've never seen him pick you up on time."

"Oh, big deal!"

"But it means something," Renee insisted. "He's cocky. . . . Oh, all right. Your mother didn't want to repeat gossip to you, but you ought to know what people think of him. A Mrs. Harris came into the dress shop—"

"Jay Harris's mother?"

"I don't know her son's name. Will you let me finish before you leap to Kyle's defense? . . . Mrs. Harris said she'd seen you with Kyle Youngman and was shocked that your mother would let you go out with a boy with his reputation."

"That's ridiculous," Anne said. "Jay Harris is the one who hangs out in pot alley—that's what they call the strip between the high school and the supermarket. And if Kyle's friendly with Jay, it's probably to help Jay straighten out. Kyle doesn't believe in doing drugs, not even pot."

"He drinks, though, and he thinks he's God's gift to women."

"Everybody in the high school has a beer now and then and it's not his fault if girls fall all over him."

"Do you drink, Anne?"

"I wander around with a beer in hand when I have to, but I don't like it."

"And hard liquor?"

"You have nothing to worry about." She launched into an earnest explanation of how remarkable it was that Kyle could pass the invisible barrier of all the cliques in school, be accepted by the jocks even though his after-school jobs kept him out of organized sports, accepted by the intellectuals because some of them had been his good friends in middle school when he'd been more grade conscious. Loners were cheered by his notice and anybody planning a party invited Kyle because his good-humored energy livened the atmosphere. ". . . and he's always ready to contribute time and money to a good cause."

"Amazing that he isn't class president," Renee said dryly.

"He could be if he wanted to be, but he has to support his car."

"How high-minded of him," Renee said.

Anne blinked. The car excuse did sound pretty lame. "He does a lot more good than other kids who get credit for it, whether you believe me or not," she said.

"Then why's he been suspended from school so much?"

"Mrs. Harris told Mom that?"

"Mrs. Harris works in the guidance office."

"Because he can't tolerate rules and regulations. The trouble is his father picks on him all the time—the way you and Grams pick on me, only worse. His father wants him to fill his big brother's shoes, the one that got killed, and Kyle's a different kind of person from his brother, but he's wonderful, Renee. If you could only treat him decently, you'd see."

"Since he won't sit down with us long enough to have a civilized conversation, I don't know when you expect me to treat him decently. Doesn't it bother you that he can't even tolerate your family for ten minutes?"

"How come you don't bring your friends home?" Anne

asked. "Mostly you meet them somewhere and we never see them."

"All right. The house is too small for private entertaining, but what does that have to do with his rudeness? Anne, this is the first boy you've dated and you're dazzled by him, but believe me, he's not the one for you. You're like a fine edition and he's common as the daily paper."

Anne laughed shortly. "That's crazy. His family lives in a nicer house in a nicer neighborhood than ours and his parents aren't divorced. If you're talking about class, he has more than I have."

"You're getting angry at me," Renee said.

"Yes, I am. You never tell me one thing about your private life. All those closed-door conferences you and mother have! If you had a boyfriend, I'd be the last to know."

"Well, I do have a boyfriend," Renee said. "Lily and I have kept it a secret, not because I don't trust you, but because we don't want Grams to know. My relationship is not an especially happy one and Grams has suffered enough in her life without anguishing over me. She lives through us, you know. She's totally devoted."

"I don't see what's so great about that. It means she expects total devotion back," Anne said, too surprised by Renee's revelation to ask questions about the mysterious boyfriend.

"Your grandmother is a loyal, loving mother whose only interest in life is making a home for her family. If you appreciate that and use a little tact, you'll find you can get along with her fine. None of us is trying to hurt you. Quite the contrary."

"Maybe you can get along by hiding things, but I'm a straightforward person, Renee."

"I know you are," Renee agreed. "That's why I don't tell

you my secrets. You won't say anything to Grams about my having a male friend, will you?"

"Don't worry, I won't. Besides, what would I tell her?"

"You want to hear the whole sad story of your aunt's disastrous love life. Okay. You're old enough—just not right now."

"Fine, and you leave me alone about Kyle, okay?"

"Touché. I'll lay off the advice. Maybe when Dodie comes, she can do something with you."

"Dodie's going to love Kyle."

"Is she? I give her credit for better sense than that."

"Let's go home," Anne snapped.

They turned at a street corner three blocks from their own where a maple was already turning scarlet. On the return trip, to make up for her attack, Renee began entertaining Anne with a story of the escapades of a young woman in her office who printed up obscene poems on the copying machine and got caught.

At the door Anne said, "I hope you're not going to poison Dodie's mind against Kyle."

"I won't say a word. Dodie can reach her own conclusions." Renee touched Anne's arm.

"It's all right, Renee. You're still my favorite aunt." They exchanged a brief embrace and went inside for dinner.

4

"Get out the brass band," Dodie's letter said.

> Dodie arrives on Sunday. Need I bring my eyelash curler or do you have one I can borrow? And what about my snorkel mask? No, don't bother answering. I'll just pack everything. Make room in your closet.
>
> The parents are leaving on Sunday too, so prepare yourself for a farewell phone call from Larry. Personally, I think he's crazy to put his business on the back burner and trail around after Mother while she puts on all these high-powered seminars. She'll be talking computer everywhere and he won't understand a word. Do you suppose he won't let her out of his sight for fear she'll run off with some other guy? He says he just feels like goofing off and I do understand that. Being lazy is such luxury. I'd make a career of it, but then how would I ever become famous?

Anne smiled as she remembered Dodie's old preoccupation with fame that summer they had spent together when they were thirteen. All her crazy costumes! Instead of trying to underplay her body, she'd called attention to it—loud-voiced, bigmouthed, a show-off. It had taken Anne a while to appreciate how bighearted and fun-loving Dodie was.

As for herself, Anne had been full of resentment at her father. It seemed unjust that the divorce had devastated her mother and allowed Larry to enjoy a shiny new bride who was both attractive and a successful executive. But by the end of that summer, Dodie and Anne were fast friends, sister-friends, and Anne had forgiven her father after all.

Even at a distance Dodie's friendship meant a great deal to Anne. Explaining her thoughts and feelings in letters to Dodie had helped Anne understand herself. Last fall she realized how lonely she was in high school when she had written,

> The only time I have anyone to talk to is during lunch. I sit with some girls I'm friendly with, but I don't really have much in common with them.

Last winter she had written,

> I'm seeing this boy Kyle Youngman. I don't know whether I like him or not, but he's a magnetic person and as popular as you are. When I see him coming down the hall, I get all stirred up. Don't ask me why. Most of our dates are disappointing. He's always dragging me places I don't much want to go, but there's something about him . . .

"Don't you dare fall in love without me around to supervise," Dodie had written back. Dodie immersed herself in her friends' love lives. Never jealous, she played the Dear Abby role with zest. Anne wished she were that generous. But in love? Until Dodie wrote that line, Anne hadn't considered that she might fall in love with Kyle. The danger of getting sexually involved with him if she continued seeing him had been what concerned her last winter. In love? She hadn't felt ready.

"Dear Dodie," she had written in June.

> I wish you lived close by so I could tell you everything about Kyle and me, and you could advise me from the vast store of your experience.

But in the summer, to her own surprise, she had fallen in love with Kyle after all, fallen into another world where nothing counted but the minutes she spent with him. It no longer mattered where he took her or who was with them, just so long as she could reach out and touch the springy hair on his arm, watch the crooked smile appear on the beautifully carved mouth, hear his heartbeat against her ear. Now her worry was how she was going to manage to spend every spare minute with Kyle and be with Dodie all the time too. Those two had to like each other. It was bad enough to have to contend with her family's dislike of Kyle without conflict between Kyle and Dodie.

"Anne, your father's on the phone," Lily called. It was Thursday night. Lily's voice was strained, still showing her pain at Larry's desertion. That lingering hurt made it hard for Anne to forgive her father no matter how much she liked and loved him.

"Hi, Daddy," Anne said, picking up the phone in the hall.

"I called to say good-bye, honey. I'll write, but I won't be talking to you much before we get back this winter."

"Are you excited about going?"

"Sure," he said. "I expect to have a ball. I've never spent any time just traveling."

"Having Dodie with me will be a ball for me too."

"I bet it will. Listen, kid, how's it going?"

"Fine."

"And with your mother?"

"She's just fine."

"Well, what's new since I last spoke to you?"

"Nothing much, Dad. I'm doing well in school."

"As usual. Think you'll win a scholarship?"

"Could be. I don't know. If not, I can go to a state school. That won't cost too much."

"Your mother and I can swing it together. How about that guy you were seeing?"

"I'm still seeing him."

"Well, when it gets serious, I want to meet him. I'm your father, don't forget."

"I don't forget, Daddy."

"I suspect your aunt and Grams have him checked out pretty carefully."

Anne laughed. "He won't set foot in the door, they've got him so checked out."

"I believe it. If your grandmother hadn't approved of me, your mother would never have married me in the first place."

"I don't let Grams rule my life."

"Good. You be strong. You're my daughter too."

"You said that already."

"Sometimes I have to remind myself. I wish we could be together more. I wish I had more involvement in your daily life."

Anne said nothing to that. She had tried to stop the divorce, and even after it she'd gone to Cape Cod that summer when she met Dodie, hoping to pry him loose from his new wife and stepdaughter.

"Well," he said. "You want to tell me anything before I leave?"

"Like what?"

"I don't know, just anything. . . . You happy?"

"Very."

"Good. That's good. Nothing better than being happy."

"Are you happy?"

"Yes, I am, Anne."

She wished him a good trip and reminded him, à la Grams, that he was calling long distance and mustn't keep the phone company in business single-handedly.

"Love you," she said before hanging up.

"And I love you, darling," he said. It made her feel good anyway, even if he was too far away to do much about it.

When Dodie's train arrived, Anne stepped away from Renee and eagerly scanned the passengers funneling onto the crowded platform. Anne hadn't seen Dodie since a brief weekend visit last spring.

A man carrying five awkwardly shaped cardboard boxes balanced on top of his considerable paunch came right behind Dodie as she got off the train.

"There you are, miss," he said, putting the boxes down on the platform. "And good luck to you. I sure hope they find the cure."

"Thanks, Mr. Glimonovitch. You're a peach. If I ever get to Utica, I'll look you up."

"You do that." He climbed back onto the train.

Dodie added a shopping bag to the stack of boxes, then

held her arms out to Anne. They fell on each other and squeezed enthusiastically.

"Dodie, I'm so glad you're here. You look wonderful."

"Why not—there's five or ten more pounds of me than last time I saw you."

"What did that man mean about a cure?"

"Hi, Renee," Dodie said, and kissed her. Then she answered Anne. "I sort of hinted I was coming here to let doctors use me as a guinea pig for some weird disease. Hey!" Dodie bellowed at a porter with a cartful of luggage. "Over here. Those are mine."

"All that?" Renee said.

"I'm moving in lock, stock and—say, how much do I have to tip? A fortune? I planned to travel light. Then I started considering possibilities. I'm counting on that big closet in your room still being half empty, Anne. I'm bunking with you, right?"

"Right."

Dodie pinched Anne's cheek and said to Renee, "I brought you a present you're going to just *love.* That's what's in the shopping bag—presents. We'll open them like a birthday party. I love parties. I love presents. Anne, I'm going to cry. I'm so glad to be here, but I'm homesick already."

"You nut!" Anne hugged her again.

Eventually they managed to tip the porter and get Dodie's belongings into the car, but not before Dodie threw her curly head back and her arms wide and yelled, "Hellooooo, Schenectady! Dodie's here."

"My God!" Renee said, first taken aback and then amused. Anne laughed and got in the car, wondering uneasily what Kyle would think of Dodie's outrageous behavior.

"I still don't see why you told that man on the train you

had a disease," Renee said as she released the hand brake and started for home.

"Well, I needed help carrying my stuff, and he wanted to tell me all about his children. He has nine, plus fifteen grandchildren. I figured I'd die of overpopulation before we got here. Nice man, though."

"You're an *enfant terrible,*" Renee said.

"That doesn't sound good. Anne, tell Renee she has to like me."

"Renee already likes you. Kyle's the one I want you to impress. He's taking us both to a clambake tonight."

"You're kidding! A clambake? I'll break out in hives. What should I wear? Renee, help me pick something to wear that'll impress Anne's guy, huh?"

"I'm sure in all that luggage there's something appropriate."

"Jeans and a T-shirt will do," Anne said.

"I have scads of T-shirts. Some of them are hilarious. This is gonna be fun . . . I hope . . . and if Kyle doesn't like me I'll kill myself."

"If Kyle doesn't like you, Dodie, you'll be in the same boat with the rest of us," Renee said. "He keeps his distance from the family."

"That's not true," Anne said.

"Kyle only appreciates females who salaam when he enters. He's got an enlarged male ego."

"Renee, you promised me you wouldn't tell Dodie anything mean about Kyle."

"I apologize. I'm in a terrible mood today. I really am sorry," Renee said.

Anne forgave her. Was the terrible mood because Renee had gone out with her "friend" last night? Anne wondered if Renee was ever going to confide in her.

As they drove home, Dodie kept up a running commentary on what she recognized from her last trip. At the shabby main street with its closed storefronts, she said, "I see the old town is still down-at-the-heels." On doctors' row she pointed out the turreted mansion turned medical office where she'd gone to get her toe X-rayed. Neither Anne nor Renee interrupted Dodie's monologue. Anne was wondering yet again how she would manage if Dodie and Kyle didn't get along and where her loyalty would lie. With luck, she wouldn't have to make a choice. They *had* to get along.

Dodie's present-giving spectacular lasted the rest of the afternoon. Grams went into shock at the false-tooth can opener Dodie had found for her in a novelty store.

"Good heavens!" was all she managed to say. Humor was not one of Grams's strong suits.

Lily glanced through the book of erotic dreams Dodie had gotten for her, said, "Dodie, you're a scream," and ran upstairs to hide it before Grams saw what it was.

Renee came out best. Her gift was a set of purple-spangled eyelashes. "I'll wear them to the next Halloween party," she said. Since Renee never went to Halloween parties, it wasn't much of a promise, but she gamely put on the eyelashes and fluttered her spangled eyelids at them.

Anne giggled at the muscleman poster Dodie presented to her next. "Isn't he gorgeous?" Dodie asked.

"Gorgeous," Anne said. "I'll hang him on the closet door so we can both admire him. But, Dodie, we've got to get dressed now. Kyle's supposed to pick us up at five."

"That means you've got hours yet," Renee said.

"He's not *always* late," Anne said, defending him. She grasped Dodie's hand and tugged her toward the stairs.

"I'll come down and model my picnic outfit for you all," Dodie promised the family.

Up in Anne's room, Dodie began to unpack, littering every surface, including floor and bed. Anne had forgotten how messy her friend was. No matter how many skirts and pants and dresses Anne hung in the big closet for her, the boxes and suitcases still appeared full.

"Dodie, you've got enough here for three people."

"I am at least three people. After all, I need wardrobes in three different sizes, and then there's my guitar and record album covers. I can't sleep without my favorite record album cover under my pillow. Are you going to hate living with me, Anne?"

"You know how I've been looking forward to it."

"You don't think I've gotten crazier than I was?"

"Just as crazy, not more."

"Anne, I love you. I have dozens of friends, but you're the best."

"Well, you and Kyle are my only friends. Now, hurry up and get dressed."

Ten minutes later Anne was ready and Dodie still hadn't decided what to wear. Luckily, Kyle was late. Disaster if he'd been sitting it out downstairs with Grams and Renee. Dodie finally chose a shirt that said RED HOT MAMA and purple jeans that emphasized her pickle-barrel shape. "I'm not dressed up enough, am I?" she asked.

"You look fine," Anne assured her. Kyle would just have to get used to Dodie's taste, which ran to purple and flash.

"I know what I need." Dodie dug out a cookie tin, which was her jewelry box, and chose a necklace of sharpened colored pencils, all hanging point down. Anne shook her head and hustled her friend downstairs.

"How do I look?" Dodie asked, posing for the family, who were still sitting in the living room.

"Colorful," Lily said, and laughed. "That's some necklace."

"It's my surefire conversation piece," Dodie said. "In case I run out of things to say."

"Have you ever?"

"Well, not yet."

"It'll mark up your T-shirt, won't it?" Grams asked doubtfully.

"Let it. I've got a zillion T-shirts. Anne, say something. You're too quiet."

"I don't *have* to say anything now you're here. All I have to do is listen."

"Am I being accused of talking too much? Quiet little old me? Renee, do you think I talk too much?"

"You've been sort of nonstop today, Dodie."

"That's because I'm so thrilled to be here. You can't imagine how much I've looked forward to being part of the family —all the nice long rap sessions we can have together. I think extended families are just super."

The bell rang. Dodie jumped and screeched, "He's here! Oh, no! Anne, don't answer the door yet. Suppose he doesn't like me. Oh, my God, I'm having a heart attack."

Not knowing how seriously to take her, the family gathered around. Each one reassured her in her own way while Anne went to open the door.

Kyle bent from the doorframe on which he'd been leaning to kiss her. "How you doing, babes?" he asked huskily. "I missed you this weekend."

"You smell good," she said.

"Stopped at a drugstore. The salesgirl squirted some male perfume on me as a joke. Like it?"

"Ummm."

"Does it get you hot?"

"Uh uh."

"No? Well, then it's not worth ten bucks. Is she here?"

"Uh huh."

"Talkative tonight, aren't you?"

"Kyle," Anne whispered. "Please like Dodie even if you don't, for my sake, please."

"For your sake, babes, I'd do anything." He let her lead him by the hand into the living room.

"Dodie, I want you to meet Kyle. Kyle, this is Dodie."

He stood there in his clean T-shirt that said REGGIE'S GARAGE and stared at Dodie. He'd known that Dodie was fat, but the actual impact of her presence seemed to surprise him. Anne knew he didn't like fat. Maybe he wasn't too crazy about purple either.

"Well, hi there," Dodie said. "I just gave Anne a picture as a joke that looks just like you."

"A joke?" Kyle asked suspiciously.

"How was I to know she dug musclemen." Dodie imitated a muscleman's stance.

"Oh." Kyle relaxed. He politely refused Lily's offer of refreshments and Grams's invitation to sit down. "Thanks, but we're late already," he said. "Maybe next time, huh?" Then he put an arm around each girl and ushered them out to his car.

"Guess we can't all sit in the front. Who's gonna squeeze in the back?" he asked.

"I don't mind," Dodie said cheerfully.

Anne watched Dodie compressing her bulk into the undersized backseat and repressed an offer to sit there instead. She didn't want to hurt Dodie's feelings.

"So you'll go to our school now?" Kyle asked over his shoulder as he zoomed off, throwing them to the backs of their seats.

"That's the plan unless they won't let me in once they see what they're getting."

"Tough on you, changing schools just for one term."

"Shouldn't be any problem. From what Anne tells me the curriculum is the same standard American Pablum I left behind."

"You must be a brain like Anne," Kyle said.

"Me? No way. I have a mental block against learning anything from a teacher I don't like. My grades go like a roller coaster."

Kyle chuckled and Anne pounced. "See? I told you you two have a lot in common."

"Lousy grades?" Kyle asked.

"No. Resistance to authority."

"Who's gonna be at this clambake?" Dodie asked. "Anybody tall, dark, and handsome for me?"

"It's a company picnic from a garage where I fill in occasionally."

"Let me guess. Reggie's Garage," Dodie said, referring to his T-shirt.

"Right. The guys invited me."

"It's good they don't mind your bringing two extras."

"Not so long as I paid them for our share. You go for clams, Dodie?"

"Love 'em, but they make me break out in hives."

"Maybe there'll be something else there you can eat," Anne said.

"Don't sweat it. I never eat much at parties."

Anne was glad Dodie couldn't see Kyle's raised eyebrows. She could have told him it was true. Dodie was a snacker, not an eater. She got her calories in bites between the refrigerator and table, or from tasting what was cooking, or sampling to see which cheese she was in the mood to eat. Dodie claimed anything not on a plate didn't count as calories.

Kyle turned into a dirt road. They drove slowly over and into craters that jolted the car chassis viciously. Dodie pretended to be riding a bucking bronco. Kyle gritted his teeth. Anne wanted to tell him Dodie was hyper because she'd just arrived, but she didn't have a chance to say it with Dodie sitting just behind them.

The road ended in a DEAD END sign. "Did you say the picnic started at five?" Dodie asked. "That means we're an hour and a half late."

"Yeah, well, if everybody shuts up, I can concentrate on getting us out of here."

Dodie got the message. Anne hoped she wasn't hurt. Kyle tried the next dirt road leading off the main paved road toward the lake. When they came to a Y intersection, he asked, "Heads or tails?"

"It's getting dark," Dodie pointed out. "Maybe the party's over."

"Look, I paid for our share of the beer and clams. They better save us some. They're probably into serious drinking by now."

"Try going right," Anne said.

"Left," Dodie said. "I get stronger vibes from that direction. Look, see this red spot on my hand? That's the clams getting closer."

"Left, the lady says," Kyle said, and proceeded to drive into the black cavern under the tree branches. The lake was the color of a dark slate under a milky sky by the time they emerged at a deserted cabin at the end of the road.

"Maybe they're playing hide-and-seek with us," Dodie said.

"This is getting ridiculous," Kyle said impatiently.

The last time Anne had seen him lose his temper, he'd been really ugly. She touched his arm and said softly, "It doesn't matter even if we don't find it, Kyle. Really it doesn't."

"It matters to me," Kyle said.

"How about a hamburger stand? My treat," Dodie offered.

"We'll try going right like Anne said."

"Maybe they gave you the wrong directions as a joke," Dodie suggested.

Kyle didn't answer. A muscle in his jaw twitched. Anne began praying they'd find the picnic quickly. The right turn was wrong too. Kyle got out and kicked a tree trunk.

"Cute, isn't he?" Dodie said dryly. Anne said nothing.

He slammed back into the car and jolted them out onto the main road, whizzing along in the darkness at a terrifying speed. For once Dodie didn't make any cracks. Anne felt like crying. Why did this night have to bring out the least attractive sides in both Kyle and Dodie? Farther down the main road Kyle tried turning toward the lake. "Last try," he said.

This time they came upon the picnic. A dozen figures showed in the car's headlights. They were sitting and standing around a campfire and two glowing charcoal grills.

"What took you guys so long?" someone greeted them.

Kyle said something obscene about the directions and everybody laughed. There was a little potato salad left and beer in the keg. Anne, who hated beer, sipped at some anyway because she was thirsty. Dodie slugged down two paper cupfuls, one right after the other, and held her empty out for more. She had no trouble mixing into the group. They teased her about her thirst and asked about her necklace. She teased back and was immediately accepted. In a little while Dodie began putting on a drunk act—at least, Anne hoped it was an act. She kept an anxious eye on her and in the process lost sight of Kyle.

When she located him again, he was being hugged by a small girl with long hair and big breasts, the kind of female he'd dated the summer he'd been a lifeguard. As usual, when he behaved this way, all Anne's self-confidence drained away. She spent the remainder of the evening loitering at the edges of the party, slapping at the mosquitos that were her only companions.

It was late when Kyle dropped them off at home. Anne and Dodie crept upstairs and into Lily's bedroom. Lily was in bed reading. "I'm sorry we kept you up, Mom," Anne said. "We had a hard time finding the party, so we got started very late."

"Did you have a good time?"

"So-so," Anne said.

"I had fun," Dodie said, yawning.

"Better get some sleep. You've got school tomorrow," Lily told her. After Anne kissed her mother good night, Lily asked her, "Anything you want to tell me, sweetheart?"

"No, Mother. Everything's okay."

Once they were in bed and the light was out, Anne asked Dodie if she'd really had a good time.

"Sure, but Kyle was a surprise. I didn't think you'd go for the macho type."

"Kyle's not macho. He puts on a big act just like you. He's actually a sensitive guy. Very intelligent, too."

"Is he? Well, maybe."

"What did you expect?" Anne asked.

"Oh, I don't know—a prep school type with horn rims and a copy of *American Scholar* under his arm."

"You didn't like Kyle?" Anne held her breath. So much depended on Dodie's answer.

"Well, he's a gorgeous hunk of man, but I can't get over you falling for Tarzan. I know you say he's sensitive, but—wow!"

Anne went stiff with disappointment.

"Are you mad at me for not being crazy about your guy?" Dodie asked.

"Why should you be crazy about him? He's my boyfriend."

"You are mad at me. I can tell."

Anne said nothing. She lay there thinking that maybe having a best friend was kid stuff. Maybe she was too old to be confiding everything in another girl. Anyway, being in love might mean the end to childish relationships. Did she wish she were thirteen again? Life had been a lot simpler then, when Chip was alive and all she had to think about was him and getting along with a new stepsister. That summer Dodie and she were in competition for Larry's affection. *He* was the type of man Dodie found attractive because he was gentle and affectionate. Well, Anne loved her father too, but she could never care passionately about so safe and soft a man. It was Kyle's dynamic quality that attracted her most. She stroked the satin skin of her breasts. If only they were larger. No lovemaking this weekend. She missed it, missed Kyle's touch. That girl at the picnic . . . Somehow there would *have* to be a time to be alone with him.

5

On Monday Dodie cheerfully followed Anne around to her classes. Morning had renewed Anne's hope that it might still work out well. Dodie seemed to have come down from the high of arrival and was acting normal—normal for Dodie. She joked with any kid near her as if they were already acquainted, as if everyone was sure to like her. By lunch period Dodie was greeting people in the hall and being greeted back. Making friends was simple, Anne saw, until she realized that something else was involved—the courage to risk rejection. Dodie had that, too.

"You're incredible," Anne said. "In a week you'll be introducing *me* around."

"Well, you never talk to anybody. I bet they think you're a snob."

Anne winced. She'd heard that people considered her cold. "I'd like to be friendly, but I'm scared," she said.

"Of what?"

"Of not being liked."

"You've locked yourself in, then," Dodie said. "Well, just remember you've got the key to your own cage."

On the school bus going home, Dodie said, "Tell me about Kyle. All I know about his family is his father gives him a hard time. What's his father do? What's he like?"

"Kyle's father? He owns Jay's Appliances, that big store downtown. He's kind of hard-nosed and bullies the whole family. Even Kyle's mother acts scared of him. She's always asking Kyle not to act up, to just go along and do what his father says."

"When did you meet his mother?" Dodie asked.

"She invited me to stay for dinner when Kyle and I were at his house. I liked her," Anne said. "She told me Kyle's her most affectionate son and that he really knows how to enjoy life. He teases her and tries to help her out. I think he's her favorite. But now that the older brother's dead, the pressure is on Kyle to be what his brother was—you know, an achiever."

"Because Kyle's the only kid left?"

"No, there are eleven-year-old twin boys. Kyle chauffeurs them around a lot. But they're seven years younger than him, and they're into sports and their friends and school. They're too busy with their own interests to care much about him. Like when Kyle and his father started yelling at each other the night I was there, the twins just looked at each other and slipped out of the room. They try to stay out of trouble, like their mother."

"Kyle's the family lightning rod."

"Yes, that's a good way to put it." Anne looked at Dodie with respect.

"I know the feeling," Dodie said. "Until Larry came, my mother never did anything but find fault with me. In a situation like that you've either got to rebel or get squashed flat."

"I told you that you and Kyle have a lot in common."

"I don't think your boyfriend thinks too much of me."

"Oh, Dodie," Anne replied. "He was just in a bad mood last night because everything went wrong."

"Could be he's jealous of how close you and I are."

"I doubt it. Kyle's a very generous, loving person," Anne said.

"Anyway, don't you worry. Kyle and I will get along if I have to get down on my knees and worship at his feet. I didn't come here to mess up your love life. Speaking of which, do you have sex with him?"

"Dodie!"

"You can tell me. We're sister-friends, aren't we? I'd tell *you* if I had a boyfriend."

"But I'm not you." Anne looked behind her to see if anyone was listening, but the bus was almost empty.

"You're so inhibited," Dodie said.

"Right, I am."

"Just tell me yes or no."

"Yes." Anne blushed and felt as naked as if she were lying on an examining table without any sheet to cover her.

"Uh oh," Dodie said. "Are you on the Pill?"

"I've been to Planned Parenthood, and that's all I'm going to say on the subject."

"At least I don't have to worry that you'll get pregnant," Dodie said. "And you're not dumb enough to consider getting married at sixteen or seventeen, even if Kyle were the marrying kind. Does your mother know?"

"No, and don't you dare tell her. She's got enough trouble."

"Is it fun having sex?"

"We don't have sex. We— Oh, Dodie, don't make me feel squirmy about it."

"It embarrasses you to talk about it but not to do it?"

"It's like something that glows in the dark. If you turn on the light, it doesn't glow."

"So *that's* what you see in him."

"I was in love with him before. I loved him when all he ever did was kiss me," Anne said defensively.

"And you think he's the one for you. Well, don't worry," Dodie said. "I'll make it my business to like him."

Grams had gone all out to make Dodie's first dinner with the family special. She had made her chicken fricassee with rice and glazed carrots and beans amandine. Renee brought home a chocolate layer cake from the bakery, and Anne made a tossed salad with homemade creamy garlic dressing.

"What a fantastic meal!" Dodie exulted, filling her plate for the second time. "My mother would die if she could see me. She thinks I should live on celery sticks. I despise celery sticks. Even glopped up with cheese dip, they taste like nothing. You're a great cook, Mrs. Pierce."

"I'm just a plain cook. I have a few good recipes is all."

"But you flavor things so perfectly."

Grams gave one of her rare smiles, revealing the false teeth she usually tried to hide. Anne stared at her, awestruck by Dodie's powers.

"You better not cook like this every night," Renee said, patting her flat stomach. "I can't afford the calories."

"You're just like my mother," Dodie said to Renee. "She thinks food is the enemy out to infiltrate her body. Me, I adore eating. So what if I never make it as Miss America. I can always star in a Fat Is Beautiful campaign. Or maybe I'll move to Africa. I read about one tribe there where they actually fatten up the royal women to make them more beautiful."

"Being overweight puts a strain on your heart," Renee said.

"What are you girls planning for this evening?" Lily asked, changing the subject. "Would you be up to a card game?"

"Sure." Dodie sounded delighted. "That would be fun. We never do anything together in my house. Here it's like a continuous party. What'll we play?"

"I think you can play hearts with five. Can't you, Grams?" Lily asked.

The telephone rang while they were doing the dishes. "I'll get it," Anne said, putting down her dish towel and running for the phone in case it was Kyle. It was.

"I gotta talk to you, Annie. Can you go for a drive with me? Alone."

"What's the matter?"

"I can't talk on the phone. I'll pick you up in ten minutes. Okay?"

"But Kyle, Dodie—"

"Pawn her off on your aunt or your mother. I need you, babes."

She could hear the urgency in his voice and agreed.

When she told them, they looked at her with varying expressions of disapproval. Mother said, "Anne, it's Dodie's first full day with you and you saw Kyle yesterday."

"He needs me," Anne protested.

"Hey, I never expected Anne to spend every minute with me," Dodie said. "Can't we play hearts without her?"

"It's a better game with four," Grams said, unexpectedly supporting Anne. No question Dodie was in solid with her.

Anne thanked Dodie gratefully and rushed outside to wait for Kyle.

She could feel his tension, see it in the way his jaw was set and his eyes narrowed. She sat beside him in his car, waiting for him to begin talking about it, but instead of pouring his heart out to her, he took her to a softball game in the park.

"Kyle, I'm a terrible softball player," she protested when she understood what he had in mind.

"It'll be dark in an hour. I gotta run off some steam."

She wanted to ask what he had routed her out of her family for if all he wanted to do was play ball. Instead she said, "I'll sit and watch until you're done."

"Come on. Don't be a spoilsport. Get in the game."

Half an hour later, when a tough-looking female yelled at Anne for missing a catch, Anne got angry. "Kyle," she hissed at him. "You should have invited Dodie if you wanted to play ball games. She's a better athlete than me. I'm quitting."

"Don't be mad at me, babes. Not tonight, huh?"

"Well, what are we doing here? I thought something had gone wrong and you wanted to talk to me."

"Just wait, will you? I got to work it out of my system."

It was his turn at bat. He hit the softball as if he wanted to demolish it. Then he threw himself violently at the bases so that Anne, now watching from the sidelines in the waning light, thought he was going to break a leg. The moon was out when the game finally ended. She didn't know whether to be furious or to laugh.

"Come on, I'll buy you a soda," he said. They drove to an ice-cream parlor clear across town. She was determined to wait for him to say something first, but her impatience got the better of her.

"You ready to talk yet?" she asked after they had finished the cones they had settled for.

"I'm getting there. How's Dodie doing?"

"Fine. She gets along beautifully with everybody. Did you like her?"

"Yeah, but it's going to be tough setting her up with a guy the way she looks."

"Who said you have to set Dodie up? She has such a terrific personality that she makes friends on contact."

"I hear you. But she sure isn't the kind of friend I expected you to have."

"She's my only friend."

"Like I'm your only guy?"

"Yes."

"You sure can pick them, Annie. Dodie's an elephant and I'm an ass." The bitter set of his beautiful mouth convinced her. He did need her here to listen.

"I almost kicked the back door out of our playroom today," Kyle began. "He hates me. Can't wait until he's seen the last of me. Without me there, it'll be peaceful. Mom and the twins will jump when he cracks the whip—until the twins get a little older."

"He must love you underneath, Kyle. He probably just can't show it."

"Bull! My father shows his feelings plain enough."

"What happened tonight?"

"Nothing—I thought I'd mow the lawn. He's been after me all week to do it. So I get out the mower and it won't start. Okay. Instead of just leaving the thing for him to fix, I decide to do him a real big favor and fix it myself. So I take the engine apart and damn if the flywheel isn't cracked! Now that's a major repair and the mower's practically an antique. So I leave the parts spread out in his workroom and trot on upstairs like a good little boy to report.

"So far this has cost me several hours of my afternoon, and if I don't get that English theme in tomorrow, she swears she's gonna fail me this time. Okay. Never mind all that. 'Who told you you could take the engine apart?' he asks me. 'You probably broke the flywheel trying to yank the parts out by brute force. That's how you wreck everything you touch.' "

Kyle stopped talking. Anne put her hand on his shoulder and rubbed the back of his neck.

"So you think he loves me, huh?" Kyle asked.

"Kyle . . ."

"Listen, princess. Just don't tell me any fairy tales."

"What did your mother say?"

"Nothing. She's so scared he'll turn around and yell at her that she lays low to avoid trouble. Pretends we're the picture of a happy family—suburban-style perfect. . . . Anyway, the way it ended, I blew my stack and said a lot of nasty things with a few obscenities thrown in. I swear, he really believes I broke that flywheel. Never mind I've always been top of my class in any shop course, fixed my brothers' bicycles for years, fix my own car, get paid to fix other guys'. No. Dad says I can't take a lawn mower apart without breaking it. It's crazy. What I ought to do is get out of the house. Set myself up somewhere so I don't have to answer to him. It would save everybody grief."

"You've got to finish high school for your own sake," she said.

"For my own sake I ought to stay and stick him for four years of college. I ought to show him just how wrong he is about me, become an engineer or a lawyer maybe."

"You could. You could do anything you want. You have the ability."

"What makes you think so?" he asked.

"I know you."

"Maybe you're wrong and the others are right. Maybe I'm a bum, Annie."

"No way."

He cupped her cheek with his hand as if she were made of precious stuff. "You're the best I've got. You know that?" He tugged at her waist and she slid across the seat. His murmurs of affection filled the spaces in her head so that the world outside disappeared. There was only the hum of love and the touch and taste and smell of it.

Tiptoeing up the stairs that night, she felt guilty. She had promised Lily she wouldn't stay out past ten on a school night and it was nearly midnight. Shameful to keep abusing Lily's trust. Anne crept through her mother's bedroom to her own as quietly as possible, but Lily's voice floated through the darkness to her. "You're so late, Anne."

Anne sat down on a corner of the shadowy bed. "I know, Mom. I'm taking advantage of your good nature. What can I say? I'd much rather have been back early, but Kyle was having a hard time and he needed to talk to me."

"And?"

"And that's all. He played some ball, too. He's feeling better now."

"It must make you feel important that he says he needs you."

"Yes, it does."

"Your family needs you too, Anne."

"I know." She was going to say she was sorry, but caught her lower lip in her teeth to stop herself. Sorry was just a plea to be forgiven one more time, and she didn't really deserve so much forgiveness.

Lily was silent, thinking; then, finally, she sighed and let it drop. "I just turned out the light a few minutes ago," she said. "I finished that John Jakes book." She yawned.

"Ummm," Anne said. Lily liked long books that took her days to read. She finished them reluctantly and immediately sought to lose herself in another. Anne understood. She had been like that herself before Kyle—B.K., as Renee put it. She had been a different person B.K. "Too good to be true," her aunt had described her once soon after they had all moved in together.

"Was Dodie good company?" Anne asked.

"Delightful. She's a darling girl. Fits right into the family as if she were one of our own. I think *we'll* enjoy having her around more than you will. What does Kyle think of her?"

"They have to get used to each other."

"Oh? A little conflict there? They both want to be first with you, I'm sure," Lily said.

"I can't imagine either of them being jealous over me, Mother. They can get a million friends. I'm the one who needs them."

"You still don't know how special you are, Annie."

"Only to you."

"Well, I know you best. . . . And you're still crazy about Kyle?"

"Why shouldn't I be? I thought *you*, at least, liked him, Mom."

"I think he's attractive. I just wish your first relationship with a boy hadn't turned out to be such a serious one."

"I'm a serious person."

"But you're still a child, even if you don't see yourself that way. You're so vulnerable and he's—"

"Mom, I'm sorry to worry you. I don't mean to. I really feel bad that I've been giving you a hard time lately. I'd rather give you pleasure. Really."

"You're always a pleasure to me. You're the best thing in my life. Don't ever think otherwise. Come give me a kiss. Do you know, this is the first talk we've had, just the two of us, in a long time?"

"I know. I'm sorry." Anne moved to the side of the bed and gave her mother a hug and a kiss in the dark.

"Listen, my darling child. I want you to stop saying you're

sorry. You don't have to apologize for anything to me. I know you have to grow up and leave the nest and all that. I want you to. All I really care about is your safety. I don't want to see you hurt in any way. And I worry about how you'll feel when your relationship with Kyle ends."

"Maybe it won't end."

"I'm not sure that's any better." Lily squeezed Anne's hand. "You are going to college, aren't you? You wouldn't sacrifice that part of your future, would you?"

"Don't worry, Mom. I'm a sensible girl."

"That's what I'm counting on. But I'm glad Dodie's here. Despite her craziness, she's got a lot of common sense. . . . Anne, you and Kyle—how physical are you together?"

Anne hesitated. Tell the truth and give Lily more to worry about, or lie? She never lied to her mother, and Lily had asked a direct question. Still— "Mother, you can trust me. I won't get in any trouble."

"Trouble?" Lily sat up straight. "I'm asking how far you and Kyle have gone. . . . Have you slept with him? . . . Oh, God, I should have known he wasn't the type to keep seeing a girl who didn't." Lily caught her lower lip in her teeth, as if to bite back her tears.

Anne said, "It's not the end of the world. I love Kyle. What's so terrible about making love with a guy you love?"

"You're too young!"

"Not in my head I'm not. You don't think it's—that it's dirty or something, do you?" Anne asked.

"No, darling, not dirty. Just the opposite. I think sex is too precious to exchange unless you're very sure that the man you love is the one you want to spend the rest of your life with. And Kyle— Oh, Anne—he's the first boy you've ever gone out with. Suppose in a few months you break up with him. Then what do you do about the next boy and the next and the one after that? If you sleep with every boy you think you're in love with, you'll cheapen the whole meaning of a sexual union. It'll become everyday dishes rather than fine china. Do you understand what I'm saying?"

"I don't plan to go to bed with every boy I meet," Anne said angrily.

"You're sixteen and you've started."

"I love Kyle. You don't believe me, but I really do."

"Are you so sure he loves you?"

"Mother, please, you're hurting me."

"I'm sorry, darling. I don't want to hurt you. I want to stop you from hurting yourself."

"Kyle and I already have a relationship. I can't stop even if I wanted to."

"No. That's the problem, you see. Once you start, how do you stop? . . . Anne, you *can.* Just tell him you've decided it's wrong, that you're too young."

"But then he'll stop seeing me."

"Oh! I thought he loved you!"

"Mother!"

"All right. Just think about it."

Anne started to go to her room, but her mother caught her arm and asked, "What have you done about precautions?"

"We use birth control."

"What kind?"

"Mother, please. I went to Planned Parenthood and Kyle uses things. It's all right."

"It's my fault," Lily said. "I should never have let you go out with him. As soon as I met him, I knew he was too experienced for you."

"Mother, you can't live my life for me. Don't be like Grams."

"Go on to bed," Lily said. "You have to go to school tomorrow. . . . Did I get through to you at all tonight?"

"Kyle's the only one. He'll be the only one until I'm married," Anne promised.

"I hope so," Lily said. "Listen, I'm not going to tell Grams or Renee, and don't you. Renee may question you. She already suspects. I think that's why she dislikes Kyle so much."

"Do you hate him too?"

"No. . . . He isn't the boy I'd choose for you, though."

"I chose him," Anne said. "And I think he's perfect for me." She went off to bed. If nothing else, it was a relief to have told her last secret to her mother. She only hoped Lily wouldn't worry too much.

6

School was to start an hour late the next morning because of a district teachers' meeting. Renee and Lily had already left for work when Anne came downstairs, followed by Dodie, who was wearing what she called her Tahitian-girl nightgown, a purple muumuu with splashy red flowers that Larry had sent her from Hawaii. Grams was watching her favorite talk show. Anne kissed her cheek and said good morning. Dodie followed suit. Grams frowned at Dodie's bare feet. "Did you forget to pack your slippers?"

"I don't own any slippers," Dodie said.

"Renee's slippers might fit you." Bare feet were unsanitary, according to Grams, and unladylike besides.

"Dodie *prefers* going barefoot," Anne pointed out. She left Grams's frown behind to follow Dodie, who was sailing serenely on toward the kitchen.

"She can be such a nag," Anne apologized to Dodie in an undertone.

"Not unless you let her. The best thing to do with a nagger

is play deaf, dumb, and blind. That's how I handle my mother when I can't retaliate any other way."

"You two still fighting with each other?"

"But of course!" Dodie said with a phony French accent. "We draw blood regularly. Same old things—food and clothes and everything else about me that she hates. It goes like this: She says I should eat breakfast to start the day off right. I say, 'When did God lay down the breakfast law?' She says, 'You wouldn't eat so much the rest of the day if you ate a proper breakfast.' I say, 'If I get the juices started first thing in the morning, they just flow harder.' Then comes dinnertime. She hides the margarine. I find it. She puts us all on breadless diets. I keep bags of cookies hidden in empty sanitary napkin boxes. She serves diet meals that starve poor Larry. I put on weight anyway. Oh, we have fun at home."

"It sounds it."

"Did I write you she wants me to see a psychiatrist about why I eat so much?"

"You said you weren't going."

"You're not kidding, I'm not!" Dodie sat with her fists under her chin and her elbows on the kitchen table, watching Anne eat her usual juice and cereal and glass of milk. "Larry thinks this half year away from my dear mother may do us both good. He's on my side, you know. He says my body is my personal business. I'd die without Larry around."

"I take it they're still happy together?" Anne said.

"They suit each other. He adores her and she adores her too."

"It's nice that he can appreciate you and your mother both," Anne said.

"Well, Larry's a loving guy, and probably the only adult I know who doesn't nag. He talks to me as if I'm his friend."

"I'm jealous," Anne admitted, sad suddenly at her distance from her father.

"Don't be jealous," Dodie said. "You're loved enough. Your mother thinks you're God's gift to her. Your aunt dotes on you. Grams too, in her way. *And* you've got Kyle."

"I don't *have* Kyle. He's not a guy you can possess."

"Well, Larry's all I've got. You shouldn't mind sharing him anyway," Dodie said earnestly. "That's one of the things that ties us together."

Anne smiled and didn't disagree, even though she felt she'd ceded Larry to Dodie rather than shared him.

Anne carried her dishes to the sink and asked shyly, "You'd be my friend anyway, wouldn't you? If we weren't tied through Larry?"

"Sure I would."

"It's nice," Anne said, "to be able to say any dumb thing I want and know you'll understand."

"That's what friends are for."

Upstairs, Dodie picked through her cookie tin to find a large black hoop earring to match the one she already had hooked into her left ear. "Did I tell you my latest ambition?" she asked.

"Now what?" Anne smiled, thinking of all the wacky things Dodie had contemplated becoming, from a fat dancer to a swami.

"I'd like to be an earth mother in a commune. There have to be communes left somewhere. But I'd need to catch me an earth father, some gorgeous guy who likes his women fat."

"You're not fat. Just—"

"Right, right," Dodie said. "I'm a gorgeous, slim sexpot who happens to have a fat physique."

She brought it up so often now—being fat, eating, dieting.

Anne wanted to ask why Dodie was so obsessed, but Dodie was talking about how she almost got expelled from school.

". . . What happened was our biology teacher left some snakes in the refrigerator, and then she got sick and nobody remembered the snakes. So they died. All I did was find them and drape them around the assistant principal's office. He's such a stiff—gives the kids a hard time for anything. Anyway, they had to fumigate his office to get rid of the smell."

"They must be missing you back home," Anne teased.

"I'm sure. I told my friends they could get whatever they want from the principal by threatening to call me back."

"We'll have to tell Kyle that story. He'll love it. He's always giving them a hard time in school."

"Zo dell me," Dodie said, playing European psychiatrist. "Vye does a good little girl like you pick out anti-authority types like us as friends, hmmm?"

Anne sighed.

"You've got sides you've never shown me," Dodie said. Her intelligent eyes studied Anne with an embarrassing curiosity.

"We're going to be late for school," Anne said quickly.

"Right-o. Let's go. One earring looks better anyway."

In the school bus Dodie said, "Oh, by the way, I'll be going home for a weekend soon. You know those costume designs I did this summer for the drama club's musical production? I wrote you, didn't I?"

"You said you were thinking of costume design as a career."

"Right. I adore clothes. And I'm mad about the theater."

"I wish I could see what you've done," Anne said.

"Then come with me. The casting director's putting me up, but I can find you a bed with someone."

"Oh, I don't think so."

"You mean you can't even leave Kyle for a weekend?" Dodie said.

"I could, but I don't want to," Anne admitted.

"You're not afraid someone will steal him away from you, are you?"

Anne shrugged and asked if Dodie had caught up on the reading for Social Studies yet. Saying anything you wanted to a friend had its limits.

Later that week Anne discovered that Dodie and Kyle shared two classes—Community Health and English Lit. II, both open to juniors and seniors. The sight of Dodie peering into Kyle's gaping mouth outside the Community Health classroom stopped Anne on her way to the guidance office one morning.

"What are you looking for, Dodie—gold?" Anne asked.

"He says he's never had a single cavity. Can you believe that this big oaf never had to sit still for the dentist's drill in his life? It's not fair."

"I told you I'm a perfect physical specimen," Kyle said, shutting his mouth to grin at her.

"You're disgusting," Dodie said. "Isn't he disgusting, Anne? He's so in love with himself. Why can't you go around hating yourself like every other normal teen-ager?"

"Normal teen-agers don't hate themselves. Only weirdos like you do."

"How would you know what's normal? The only person you can judge anything by is yourself."

"True, I'm a superior specimen. You got a point there, Dodie." He showed all his perfect teeth in an outsize smile and sparkled his eyes for good measure.

"I'm so glad you two are learning to appreciate one another," Anne said, tickled by the teasing.

Through the glass door on Friday, Anne saw Dodie dancing

in the audiovisual resource room, whose only other occupant was Kyle. All Dodie's solid fat flowed like waves in time with the rhythms. She looked so graceful and featherlight that Anne stepped into the room and applauded. The tape came to an end and a slow song started. Dodie became a dazzled ballroom dancer, playing up to her imaginary partner. Anne tiptoed over to where Kyle was poking through the tape-catalogue drawer and hugged him.

"Isn't she sensational?" Anne asked.

"She'd be better if she'd get rid of some flab."

"I heard that, Kyle Youngman," Dodie said. She stopped dancing and joined them.

"*You* look for the tape we need," he said to her, and yawned. "It's your idea anyway."

"Tape for what?" Anne asked.

"Background for a poem. We're doing a dramatic reading together in English."

"Robert Frost's 'Home Burial.' It's the saddest poem you ever heard, Anne," Dodie said.

"Dodie's doing the farm wife staring out the window at the graveyard," Kyle put in, "and I'm the male chauvinist husband who doesn't get it. I don't think much of the typecasting."

"You'd rather be the farm wife?" Dodie asked.

"You'll be a smash hit," Anne said. "Isn't it nice that you have two classes together?"

"Oh, sure—fate has thrown us together." Dodie hammed it up, clasping her hands and batting her eyelashes at Kyle.

That night Renee asked Anne, "What made Dodie decide to go on a diet?"

"I didn't know she had."

"Well, she's either dieting or sick. I haven't seen her take a second helping lately. Hasn't she said anything to you, Anne? Funny. I'd think she'd be so proud of her willpower."

When they were getting ready for bed that night, Anne asked, "Dodie, are you on a diet?"

"Shhh. Don't say anything," Dodie said. "If my stomach gets word, it'll revolt."

"But why . . . ?"

"Anne, every pound I've ever lost has been attended by fanfare, promises, gnashing of the teeth, hoopla, and failure. This time it's all very hush-hush. My subconscious is doing its thing without interference from me."

"I understand . . . I think." She wondered if Kyle had anything to do with the diet.

As if she were reading Anne's mind, Dodie said, "Your rotten boyfriend really gets to me sometimes. Today he looks at me and goes, 'What do you look like under all that lard?' 'I'm a living doll,' I tell him. 'Yeah?' he goes. 'How d'ya know?' Anne, don't you think I have a cute nose? I mean, it's short and it turns up at the end kind of cute like, doesn't it?"

"It's an adorable nose, Dodie. You have a very pretty face."

"Not as pretty as yours. Even if I were skinny, I'd never look cool and elegant like you. Walking down the hall, you stand out, as if you're all alone in the crowd." Dodie sounded wistful.

"I *am* all alone in the crowd," Anne said, but Dodie wasn't consoled.

"You ought to go in for modeling. You could make a mint," she said.

Anne shook her head. Standing around showing off clothes or the shape of her bones didn't interest her. What she dreamed of she would never admit to Dodie or Renee or to anyone who expected a girl to be ambitious. She wanted to become the well-loved center of some successful man's life, the mother of wonderful children, a community leader. It was such a staid, conventional dream that Grams would have approved, and Anne was a little ashamed of it. Sometimes when she projected herself into the future more realistically, she would see herself devoted to books as a librarian, a researcher digging into dusty files, a teacher, a salesperson in a bookstore. Except that that kind of job seemed only possible, not joyful. Joy depended on being married to someone she loved.

She could trace the image of the accomplished wife back to Lily's friend from predivorce days. That woman's life had seemed ideal to Anne then. Although now she was experienced enough to wonder if Lily's friend had really been as fortunate as she seemed or as happy as she pretended. Was that role even possible for a woman anymore? There would have to be a certain kind of man to make it possible. Anne tried to imagine Kyle as a wealthy lawyer, as that woman's husband had been. No image formed. Kyle's energy wasn't directed yet. Even he didn't know which way he'd go, and en route his girl would have to live in a trailer and work as a waitress, live in an old house with six strangers, make do with nothing but hope. No matter. One thing Anne knew for certain was that she'd be happy as long as she was with Kyle.

After all Anne's worrying about how Dodie and Kyle would get along and how Dodie could be included in weekend activities, Anne was amused by the turnabout when Dodie and Kyle included *her* in an invitation they'd received to go sailing that Saturday.

"See," Dodie explained, "Kyle used to date this girl Sue Ann's older sister, but she's in college—the sister. So Sue Ann knows him, and then when I started talking sailing to her—

Sue Ann's in English with us—she invited us up to her summer camp."

"I see. I think. But isn't it too cold for sailing?" Anne looked at Kyle, who was leaning against the wall outside her homeroom, letting Dodie do all the talking.

"Not yet," Dodie said, too eager to let Kyle answer. "Sue Ann says it's gorgeous up there at Sacandaga now. They have two sailboats—a Sunfish and an O'Day. Oh, Anne, I know you hate sailing, but it would be such fun to teach Kyle, and he won't go unless you come too."

"No problem. I'll go and just watch."

"Listen," Kyle said. "I'll be with you, babes. You won't drown with me around."

"I won't drown with Dodie around either. She already saved my life in the water once when we were thirteen."

"Okay, so you've got nothing to worry about," he said.

She didn't argue with him. She'd see how she felt about it when she got there.

For once Kyle picked them up on time, which was fortunate because Dodie was wearing herself out by hopping up and down in excitement. "I adore sailing. I just adore it," she said. "I'd give my eyeteeth and two molars to belong to a sailing club. Larry's promised me, but summers fly by so fast. Boy, I can't wait to get Kyle out on that lake. For once I'm going to show *him* a thing or two."

"Not for long, I'll bet. He's not going to let you run the show," Anne warned.

"Yeah, you're right. He's got to be boss, doesn't he? That's the worst thing about him. You know, he's really a very bright guy, but he just *has* to get the teacher's back up. He's more anti-authority than I ever was."

"I know."

Dodie shook her head and laughed at herself. "Here I am

lecturing you on your own guy." She gave Anne a hug and went back to hopping.

Kyle was on a high too. "Can you believe this day?" he said after they piled in the car. "It's got to be eighty degrees out."

"Except that the leaves are all gold and red, you'd swear it was midsummer," Dodie exulted.

Anne smiled, enjoying their good humors.

She was thinking that after the kiddies had had their sailing fun, it would be nice if she and Kyle could go off alone somewhere. Having Dodie around all the time had hampered their lovemaking. Last night on the phone Kyle had said that he was feeling deprived. She had agreed that this weekend, somehow, they'd get some privacy.

Now, in the car, Kyle asked her, "Why so quiet, babes?"

"I'm being happy. It's so nice my favorite people like each other."

"Like is not the word," Dodie said. "Your big oaf drives me crazy. I keep wanting to slug him one."

"You're just mad because I got kicked out of class yesterday instead of you," Kyle said.

"Yeah, I had to sit there and take that dumb test while you got to hang out in the principal's office. What'd he say to you anyway?" Dodie asked.

"Oh, the usual. I better behave if I want to graduate."

"Did you write for any college applications yet, Kyle?" Anne asked.

"My mother took care of it. She figured I wouldn't get around to it, and Dad's been after me."

"Which means, of course, you won't fill any applications out, right?" Dodie said.

"I might. How about you, Dodie? You've racked up a few dirty D's too. That going to keep you out of Harvard?" Kyle asked.

"Yeah, but my PSAT score will be so super they'll come begging me to take early admissions."

Kyle laughed. "Sure," he said, and then more seriously: "Could be I'll make 'em wait for me while I try working first. What about you, Annie? When it's your turn, are you going off to Vassar or Smith or someplace like that?"

"Maybe I'll go to SUNY. That way I can stay here with you."

"Don't count on it. I'll probably head west next summer. There's gotta be more exciting places for me to work in than Schenectady."

Next summer? Wouldn't they still be together? She looked at Dodie with such clear distress that Dodie suggested quickly, "How about you and me going backpacking around Europe next summer, Anne?"

Anne shook her head. That wasn't what she wanted. "Where would I get the money? Besides, my family would never let me do that."

"You'll be seventeen. That's old enough."

"Grams won't think so."

"I forgot Grams," Dodie said.

The fizz had gone out of the day for Anne. Nothing was permanent—not Kyle, not even Dodie. Dodie would go back home after December, back to her other friends who could travel with her. And Kyle? Who knew what he would do? When they got to the lake, she chided herself: no sense ruining a beautiful day worrying about tomorrow. Today they were both hers. She put on a smile to greet the look-alike brother and sister who came running out of the small green clapboard cottage toward them.

"We've been waiting for you. The wind is just fantastic today!" Sue Ann said.

It was true. Anne looked apprehensively at the trees sweeping their heavy limbs about. Everything that could move was in motion. There were whitecaps on the lake. "I don't think this is my kind of sailing weather," she said.

"This is when it's best," Dodie said. "Come on, Anne. Kyle and I are both good swimmers." She began bouncing again, and Kyle looked like a barely restrained racehorse.

"You guys enjoy yourselves. I'll sit on the shore and have a ball watching you."

"Hey, Annie!" Kyle began.

"Please, Kyle. I really will have a much better time and so will you. I get scared when the boat heels."

"Do you want the O'Day or the Sunfish, Dodie?" Sue Ann asked impatiently.

"Sunfish. That way Kyle can be captain when he gets the hang of it, and it won't matter if we tip over."

"You just made my brother happy," Sue Ann said. "Okay, let's go."

"Can I help?" Anne asked, following them to the short pier.

"We're all set. There's soda in the cooler and a lounge chair if you want to drag it down from the lawn," Sue Ann said over her shoulder. Her brother was already in the O'Day. She hopped in after him. They released the line that tethered them to the shore and were gone. Seeing them heel until they had to hike their bodies way out over the edge to keep the boat from tipping into the lake, Anne was glad she had chosen to stay put. Dodie and Kyle were already taking off in the Sunfish. Anne gasped at the speed with which the O'Day zipped away.

"Be careful," she yelled at Dodie and Kyle, but they only waved. They were practically sitting in the water. Dodie was talking fast, probably trying to teach Kyle everything she knew in the first run before he got bored and wanted to try it himself. The red-and-white-striped sail was soon so far into the middle of the lake that Anne couldn't distinguish their figures below it. They changed course once, twice, and without surprise she saw the Sunfish flip over. In a few minutes it was righted, and they were off again, racing down the lake after the O'Day. She remembered when Dodie had taken Chip sailing that summer three years ago. How he had loved it! The longing to have him beside her swelled painfully. When it subsided, she stretched out on the warm wooden pier and closed her eyes. The sun, the sounds of water clapping on the wooden pilings, and wind sifting through leaves made her drowsy.

"You're my special girl, Annie," Kyle had said during last night's phone call.

"What makes me special?"

"You rest me," Kyle had said. It was such an odd answer. Did he mean she put him to sleep? "You rest me." Now in the sunshine with her eyes closed, she thought: He loves me. I'm sure he loves me even if he doesn't know it. Do I love him? Sixteen was young, but she felt old enough to commit herself to him forever, except—suppose it meant she had to give up college. Was he worth it? He was an escape from the suffocating love of her family. He gave her joy where they gave her merely security. They bound her with restrictions and demands and mired her in guilt. All he asked was that she belong to him. Half asleep, Anne imagined Kyle sitting beside her, looking at her, his hands touching her. . . .

When she opened her eyes, he stood over her dripping cold water onto her warm body. "You fell asleep in the sun, lazybones," he said.

"You weren't gone long."

"Sure we were. I sailed her and Dodie sailed her. We did most of the lake."

"Was it fun?"

"Great! I don't know if I'd like it without all that wind, though. It could get boring."

"Where's Dodie?" She looked around, saw the sailboats leashed to shore again, but no Dodie or Sue Ann or her brother.

"They're up at the cottage looking at Sue Ann's trophies. Do you want to go look?"

"Not particularly."

"Good. I don't either." He sat down next to her and took her in his arms. His body was cold and wet against her sun-warmed skin, but she held him tightly and the taste of his mouth on hers was good. Little trills of desire curled through her, roused by his lips and his warm breath and his hands as they caressed her back.

"Trophies!" Dodie's voice said loudly. "Sue Ann and her brother have cleaned up all the races on the lake. You kids should go see." Her voice sounded odd.

Anne looked at her. Dodie's face was red—from sun? From embarrassment? Did it bother her to see Anne and Kyle kissing?

"I don't think they're going to feed us anything. Are you guys hungry?" Dodie asked.

"Moderately," Kyle answered, nuzzling Anne's neck.

"Maybe we ought to thank them and start back," Dodie said.

"Fine by me. How about you, Annie?"

"Yes, let's go." She stood up. "I'm starving."

"Let's stop in for some hamburgers. My treat," Dodie said.

That night in bed Dodie said plaintively into the darkness, "You're so lucky, Anne."

"You mean because of Kyle?"

"Because you're pretty."

"Oh, Dodie! That's dumb. Pretty! Anybody can be pretty."

"He wouldn't hold you like—the way he was holding you—if you weren't pretty. I wish some guy would want me like that."

"Dodie Amesley, you know you're a sexy, gorgeous creature. You'll get your guy."

"Not unless I take off about fifty pounds."

"So do it."

"I'm trying, but I've never been able to stick to a diet in my life. I make pacts with myself and break them. All it takes is some disappointment or a would-be funny comment from somebody and I start eating myself fatter than I was before. I don't even know what I'd look like if I weren't fat. Maybe I'd be ugly anyway."

"No," Anne said earnestly. "I'm positive you'd be beautiful, if—well, you're attractive now, so of course you'd be beautiful."

"My mother is a pretty woman. I don't think she's ever been a pound overweight in her life. But I look like my father instead of her. You know that picture of him in uniform she gave me to remember him by? He was good-looking, wasn't he, Anne?"

"I wish you wouldn't think looks are so important."

"They are. Anyway"—Dodie yawned loudly—"we had a ball out on the lake. Kyle's as much of a nut as I am."

Anne was disturbed, touched by Dodie's confession of longing and disturbed by the ugly truth in what she said. Surely, Dodie's physical self wasn't going to keep her from being loved. Pounds couldn't be that important except that Anne knew they were to Kyle. Well, maybe wanting to be desirable would help Dodie stay on a diet. How nice it would be for her to have a guy she cared about. Then Anne wouldn't have to feel guilty about having Kyle.

"You going to miss me when I go back home next weekend?" Dodie asked sleepily.

"Very much."

"Liar. You won't miss me at all. You can devote yourself completely to old sex-on-the-hoof while I'm gone."

"Dodie! You know I love being with you better than anyone else in the world."

"Except Kyle."

"Well, you can't expect me to prefer you to him."

"Heavens, no!" Dodie mocked. "No girl can ever be as important to another girl as a guy is. Man and woman is the primary relationship."

"Don't be jealous," Anne begged.

"Well, I can't help it."

"Anyway, man and woman isn't really the primary relationship."

"Sure it is," Dodie said. "Adam and Eve came first and sexual attraction is strongest, especially at our age."

"How about mother and child?"

"Who comes first, your mother or Kyle?"

Anne didn't answer. It struck her that she didn't know, and suddenly she was glad Dodie was going away for the weekend.

7

"Dodie's really integrated into our family amazingly well. It'll be dull without her," Renee said to Anne in the car after delivering Dodie to the train station Thursday night. "But it must be difficult for you."

"You mean because of Kyle?" Anne asked. "That's working out. He's been pretty good about including Dodie in things. Anyway, she's made so many friends at school that she's not dependent on me."

"That's not what I mean," Renee said. "What I'm talking about is her crush on Kyle."

"Dodie's my best friend. She'd never let herself fall for my guy," Anne said in surprise.

"Don't fool yourself, sweetie. Nobody controls crushes. They just happen."

"You're crazy, Renee. What makes you think she's fallen for him?"

"The way she looked at him."

"That's all? A look?"

"Well, tell me why she's suddenly decided to lose weight," Renee said.

"Dodie's my friend. She'd never—"

"She can't help herself. You know how I love your mother. Well, would you believe I had a secret crush on your father for years?"

Anne stared at Renee and said, "No! On my father?"

"All the time your mother was dating Larry, I used to dream that he'd dump her for me," Renee said. "Oh, I knew I didn't have a chance. Lily was an adorable girl and I was a homely kid, but that didn't stop me from wanting him. I even felt noble because I urged your mother to marry him. With all good intentions, Grams and I pushed Lily into marrying a man she didn't love just because *we* thought he was a prize. Well, he is, but not for your mother. Anyway, that's how I can read Dodie so well."

Overwhelmed by Renee's revelations, Anne focused on Dodie. That expression on Dodie's face when she saw Kyle and Anne embracing at the lake—the way Dodie had flirted with Kyle in school. "If you're right, what can I do about it?" Anne asked her aunt.

"Not a thing," Renee said. "Just be understanding. It isn't easy being the ugly stepsister."

"Poor Dodie," Anne said.

"And whatever you do, don't humiliate her by letting her know *you* know how she feels about Kyle."

"Did Mother know about you and Larry?"

"Not for years. I didn't confess until she told me about the divorce."

"You're really good at keeping secrets."

"That I am."

Renee turned into their own driveway. Anne released her seat belt, preparing to leave the pale blue confessional of

Renee's car. "It's funny," Anne said. "Dodie and I competed for my father when we first met. That was easier to fix, though. We could share a father."

"Did you? I thought what happened was Dodie got him and you got Dodie as a consolation prize."

Anne frowned, at the sharp-edged truth. "Anyway, I'm not sharing Kyle—not with any other girl," she said.

After dinner, Renee drove off to meet a friend. Grams had the television going while she worked at a jigsaw puzzle spread out on a bridge table. Lily was lost in a romantic novel. Anne went up to her room to do some schoolwork. She opened her books around her on the bed and tried to begin, but her mind kept turning over what Renee had said. Apparently there were still secrets, still things she didn't know about the people closest to her. How could she ever be expected to understand life when people kept secrets from her?

She remembered that it had been Larry who told her about the divorce. He'd said all the standard things a parent is supposed to say to a child. "Your mother and I are not happy with each other anymore. We still love you more than anything, but we can't live with each other. Just remember we both love you even if we've stopped loving each other." It had scared her to find out you could stop loving someone. If they didn't love each other anymore, why *couldn't* they stop loving her?

Always, Anne had blamed her father for the divorce. Even though she never said anything, she had been sure it must be his fault. Lily was so gentle and needed him so much. Lily had suffered from being left to make a living for herself and take care of her daughter alone. Now Anne wondered. Had Lily been the victim or not? As if the question had summoned her, Lily poked her head around the door just then. "You still working, angel?"

"Mom, can I talk to you for a while?"

"What a question. Of course you can." Lily made the bed sag as she settled down, curling her legs up under her. She was plump—not fat like Dodie, but plump in the body and face. Her arms and legs were still slim and the lovely eyes, the pert nose, and bow-shaped lips were still there in her puffy face. But only in old photographs could Lily be called pretty. "What did you want to talk about?" Lily asked eagerly.

"Renee told me something in the car this evening. She said you weren't in love with Dad when you married him."

"Did she say that? Well, I wasn't wildly in love. I mean, my eyes didn't light up when I saw him and he didn't make my heart beat faster, but I was very fond of him."

"Then why did you marry him?"

"Because all the mad passions I'd had for other boys never lasted, and Larry was so sweet . . ."

"And Renee and Grams talked you into it?"

"He talked me into it. They just encouraged me. Anne, I did love your father. We had a good enough marriage."

"So what happened?" Lily shrugged, but Anne demanded, "Tell me."

"What happened was Louis Adelman moved next door to us," Lily said.

"Who was Louis Adelman? You mean that funny-looking guy who used to come over all the time? The one who played the trumpet?"

"He wasn't funny-looking. He was a little bald and very romantic. He's why your father divorced me. I wanted to marry Louis."

"You mean you had an affair with him?"

"Yes. I got carried away. I—Oh, Anne, I'm sorry." Lily covered her face with her hands.

"Why didn't you tell me before?" Anne asked, thinking of all the years when she'd blamed her father for the divorce.

"Because I need you," Lily said. "And I was afraid."

"It wasn't right to let me blame Daddy all this time."

"He never said anything to you about Louis?"

"You know he didn't."

"Larry's a very decent man. It's true I learned to appreciate him too late, and it's true I did a terrible thing to him, but Anne, if your father had been willing to forgive me, I would have gone back to him. He wouldn't take me back. His pride —Anyway, he's happy and I've gotten my comeuppance, haven't I?"

"Oh, Mother, I'd never think that. But why do we have all these secrets? All the talking we do, and we still have all these secrets from one another."

"Would you have stayed loyal to me if you'd known why your father divorced me?"

"I love you, Mother."

"But would you have forgiven me?"

"I think so. I don't know." She had loved her father too. The hurt that showed on Lily's face made Anne hurry on. "Louis Adelman," she said. "I just don't see how you could have preferred that funny little man to Daddy."

"Why did you fall for Kyle instead of some other boy? It just happens, doesn't it?"

Anne drew a deep breath. She had fallen for Kyle because he was the most wonderful boy around.

"And that's why I worry about you," Lily continued. "I don't want you following in my footsteps. I want you happy and successful and fulfilled. Forgive me, Anne, but Kyle's not going to bring you any of that."

"You don't know Kyle, Mom. There's much more to him than you see, and I'm not a fool."

"You're a sensible girl—but not in love you're not sensible. You're not my child for nothing." Lily held out her arms. Anne embraced her mother. Poor Lily! Larry was happily married. He had a good life. What did Lily have? Her thousand-page novels, Renee and Grams, plus a daughter who wasn't doing much for her peace of mind these days.

In bed that night Anne brooded over how unfairly she had blamed her father all these years. She ought to write and tell him that she now knew the divorce hadn't been his fault, but how could she without sounding disloyal to her mother? What had happened in her parents' relationship wasn't her business to judge, after all. Better to wait until she had her father alone sometime and tell him when she could watch his reaction and hear his response.

She thought about the strangeness of it all. Renee and Lily and Larry had made one triangle and now Dodie and Kyle and she made another. It was frightening that sexual attraction had the power to break down even the strongest loyalties.

8

To please her, Kyle had consented to come for dinner that Friday night while Dodie was away, but as six o'clock approached, Anne began to wish she hadn't asked him.

"When did you tell him we eat, Anne?" Grams asked.

"Don't worry. He'll be here any minute." Anne crossed her fingers behind her back.

"Why should he be here on time tonight when he never is any other night?" Renee asked. The tracks between her eyes meant she'd had a hard day at work and was feeling irritable. Her lips were pursed just like Grams's.

"Listen, he's only coming because he wants you all to like him. I convinced him you would once you got to know him," Anne said.

"Poor guy," Lily offered, wriggling her stockinged toes as she rested her feet on the couch. Her pumps stood ready to be slipped on when Kyle arrived. Everyone was all dressed up and waiting. The kitchen table was set with a good linen cloth, the one Grams saved for special occasions. Anne knew she should feel honored that Grams had used it tonight, but she also knew the more formal this evening was, the less relaxed Kyle would be. The smell of Grams's chicken fricassee permeated the downstairs. Anne looked anxiously out the living room window, willing Kyle's aged car to appear.

"Whatever you do," she said, "please don't ask him what he wants to be when he grows up."

"Anne!" Lily chided. "Don't you think we know how to treat a guest?"

"I'm just telling you. He doesn't like being asked. He's not sure of what he wants to do, and his father keeps pushing him."

"It's six o'clock," Grams said.

"That clock's fast, Mama," Lily said.

The shriek of a car wheeling to a sudden stop in their driveway followed by the slam of a car door sounded like salvation to Anne. She flew to open the door for him.

"Almost didn't make it. The points were wet," Kyle said, and kissed her on the lips. "How do I look?" he whispered.

"Gorgeous," she whispered back. He had on an open shirt under a sports jacket and proper pants.

"I don't need a tie, do I?"

"You look fine."

"Here." He produced the paper cone with protruding stems from behind his back like a proud magician.

"Oh, Kyle, how nice!" She stood on tiptoe to whisper in his ear, "Give them to Grams."

"Do I gotta?"

"Yeah, you gotta."

"Okay, here goes." He took a deep breath, pulled his shoulders back, and strode into the living room, where the three women sat looking up at him. On came his winning grin. "Hope I'm not late, ladies."

"Right on time," Lily said with a smile.

"Well, I brought you some flowers." He held them out neutrally, presenting them to the group at large. Lily took the bouquet and thanked him. He stood grinning while she peeled back the wrapping paper to reveal a dozen giant white spider mums.

"Oh, how beautiful! Aren't these glorious, Mama?"

"Ummm, nice," Grams said. "I never saw ones that large."

"They're handsome," Renee said. "I'll get the big cut-glass vase down from the closet."

After the flowers were set in water and placed on the end table in front of the window and everybody had given them another round of praise, Grams announced dinner. Kyle asked to be excused so he could wash his hands, which were grease-streaked from working on his car. As soon as Anne closed the door behind him, she remembered that Grams had put out the hand-embroidered linen fingertip towels. A quick glance over her shoulder assured Anne nobody was in the kitchen yet. "Kyle," she hissed through the door. "Don't use the linen towels."

"Too late." He stuck his head out the door. "Here, you better hide the evidence." The towel he handed her as he sauntered out was adorned with black smudges. His shirt was equally marked where he'd wiped his hands on it. The jacket had hidden the grime before. Now the jacket hung from his finger.

"Put your jacket back on," she said.

"They already saw me in it."

"Kyle, please."

"Okay, okay."

Kyle got the side of the kitchen table with his back to the refrigerator. Grams sat with hers to the stove. Lily and Anne had the sink between them, and Renee had an odd corner, squeezed between dish closets and the back door.

"Hope you don't mind eating in the kitchen, Kyle," Renee said. "We had to convert the dining room into a bedroom for Mother. She can't make the stairs with her bad hip."

"I like eating in the kitchen," Kyle said. "It's more—"

"Cozy," Anne supplied, and Kyle nodded.

"Well, it's not the way I'm used to entertaining guests," Grams said. "But you learn to make do. I hope you like chicken, Kyle."

"Oh, sure. I'm not a fussy eater." He picked up his spoon and set to on his grapefruit. Anne hoped nobody noticed that he hadn't put his napkin in his lap.

"You're a senior, aren't you?" Renee asked Kyle.

"Sort of. I had some differences of opinion with a couple of teachers last year so I've got some makeup to do, but I'm in no hurry to graduate."

Anne saw Renee looking at Kyle's hands. He was holding the spoon clenched in his fist instead of lightly held between his fingers, and worse, now his left elbow came up and rested on the table. Renee was a stickler for proper table manners. She even picked on Lily and Anne for sloppy habits. Anne rose to clear away the plates with the grapefruit rinds.

Kyle tried a conversational opening. "My mother says she knows you, Mrs. Busca. She says you helped her find a dress for my cousin's wedding."

"Oh, yes. Was that your mother, Kyle? I recognized the last name, but I know there are several Youngmans in town, and she doesn't look like you. She's so petite, a lovely figure."

"Yeah, well, she works at it—spends half her time at the health spa."

"Well, it shows."

"Yeah," Kyle said. "She keeps herself looking good. My Dad likes it that way."

"Lily's only working as a saleslady temporarily," Grams said. "Just to see if that kind of business suits her. She had her own business before—an antiques store."

"Oh, really?" Kyle said without much interest.

"There's nothing wrong with being a salesperson, Grams," Anne said, knowing that in Grams's mind being a salesperson gave her daughter a lower social standing than Kyle's mother, who could afford to spend her time at a health spa.

"I never said there was," Grams said, and began levering herself from her chair.

"I'll serve the chicken, Mama," Renee said. "You sit still."

"You look like an athlete," Lily said to Kyle, taking her turn with the conversation. "Are you a sports enthusiast?"

"Sure, I like sports—not the competitive kind, though. I mean, I never got into football or baseball or basketball. That Little League kind of stuff turns me off. I was on the ski team for a while, but then I dropped out. I'd rather do sports just for the fun of it, you know?"

"That's nice," Lily said. "So many kids are too competitive."

"Right. Sports are best for burning off energy. I like moving, doing anything fast." He illustrated enthusiastically by pumping his arms in the air, thereby jiggling the table and the china and glasses crowded on it. "Oops, sorry," he said.

"No problem," Renee said. "This kitchen is a bit of a tight fit."

"Good thing Dodie's not here tonight," Kyle said.

"Don't you like Dodie?" Renee asked.

"Oh, she's great, a terrific kid. I just meant because of the space."

"This house was big enough to raise two children in," Grams said. "It's suited me for forty years."

"It's a neat house," Kyle said. "These old places have a lot of character."

"I suppose your house is larger?" Grams asked.

"You mean my father's house? Well, it's a little bigger, yeah. There were four of us kids before my brother died, so we needed more space."

"Anne told me you had lost a brother too," Lily said. "She says you knew Chip—" Her voice caught on her son's name.

"Chip was a great kid. Yeah. I felt bad when— Yeah, that was really too bad."

"Chip was a good boy," Grams said.

"The best," Renee said. "We all miss him."

"I know. I know how it is." Kyle had finished his chicken and hadn't yet told Grams how good it was.

Anne prompted him by saying, "The chicken's delicious, Grams."

"Kyle, will you have some more?" Grams asked him.

"Oh, no thanks. That was plenty for me."

Silently, Anne urged him to compliment Grams, but her message didn't get through, and Grams remained purse-mouthed and unappreciated.

Later, after they'd discussed last night's news broadcast and after Anne and Lily had done the dishes with Kyle's help, and after it was too late to win any points with Grams, Kyle said to her, "Thanks for inviting me. It was a really good dinner."

Anne walked him to his car, shivering in the cold night.

"Well, do you think I improved my ratings any?" he asked her.

"Sure you did," she lied. "You were perfect."

"Oh, face it, Annie. They don't like me, and I'm not too

crazy about them either, and no amount of chitchat is going to change that."

"My mother likes you."

"Your mom's a sweetheart, like you. The other two are uptight. Listen, I was a good boy tonight, but no more of this for a while, huh?"

"But, Kyle—"

"The folks are clearing out tomorrow, taking the twins and going to visit some friends for the weekend. We have my house all to ourselves."

"I don't think that's a good idea. What if they walked in unexpectedly or if some neighbor told them—"

"Hey, that's silly."

"No, it isn't."

"Look, I'll call you tomorrow. Get in the house before you freeze to death." He kissed her. "Don't you want to be alone with me?"

"Oh, Kyle, you know I do. But not at your house."

When she asked what they thought of him, their answers were guarded. "He's an attractive boy," Lily said.

"His table manners could use some improvement," Renee commented.

"Grams?" Anne asked. "Wasn't it nice of him to bring the flowers?"

"I can't say I thought too much of him," Grams said. "He looks fast to me."

"God!" Anne said. "There's no pleasing you. And besides, I don't see why I have to please everybody anyway." She raced upstairs, propelled by her anger. She was in bed, awake and still angry, when Lily came into her room.

"Why do we have to live with them, Mom? I can't stand

having my life ruled by three different people. They're not my parents. You are."

"They mean well and they love you very much."

"They're wrong about Kyle. Mother, I love Kyle."

"I know," Lily said. "But the thing is, I'm happier here than I was when we were trying to make it alone. I need my mother and sister. And they're not all wrong about Kyle, darling. I like him, but he's not— Well, he worries *me* too."

Anne was so angry she didn't trust herself to speak. They were suffocating her with their concern. How was she ever going to be an independent person if she had to live not just by her mother's judgments but by Grams's and Renee's as well?

"Only you would come up with a place like this," Anne said the next day when Kyle produced the tepee hidden in a clearing surrounded by tall trees at the end of a dirt road. He and Dodie! They always had a friend willing to share a handy boat or vehicle or shelter. The tepee fellow, according to Kyle, was a doctor's son and would-be ascetic who had moved out of a three-story mansion, with sixteen rooms and a live-in maid, into woods his uncle owned. This weekend he was visiting his girl friend in Cincinnati.

"He's a character," Kyle said.

"All your friends are characters."

"I like all kinds of people."

"I know. You can get along with anybody," Anne said.

"Even you."

"Even me."

Now they were lying on Kyle's sleeping bag, their bare toes to the wood stove, which kept the tepee warm even on this frosted October afternoon. "Now, isn't this nice?" Anne coaxed, aware that he was still annoyed because she wouldn't go to his house. "It's so cozy here. I love it."

"Except I'm hungry and there's no refrigerator, and if we have to use that outhouse back there, we'll freeze our butts off."

"I wouldn't have felt right making love in your house."

"Nobody would've walked in on us."

"I like my nice-girl image."

"Nice girls have sex too, although I don't know any nice girls who like sex as much as you do."

"Only with you."

"Right. You're mine. All mine." He fell upon her, devouring her with kisses and snuffling, growling noises that made her laugh and reawakened the excitement so that soon they were making love again. They so rarely had lain completely naked like this with space and time enough to enjoy each other without worrying about being discovered. The freedom from anxiety exhilarated Anne. She felt like a new person. Off with the shell of shy reserve that kept her apart from people! His eyes and hands desiring her made her feel beautiful.

Finally he drew her close against him and fell asleep. She lay still so as not to disturb him and smiled contentedly, watching the fire. The tepee creaked in the wind that soughed through the bare, rattling branches, but she felt safe. The afternoon of the tepee, she thought. When other experiences were forgotten, this one would remain in her memory. She could imagine asking him years from now, "Do you remember the afternoon of the tepee?" And he would answer with a kiss that held all the reassurance she would ever need.

Still, when he woke, yawning noisily, she asked him, "What time is it?"

"What does that matter?"

"I can't keep strolling in after midnight. You don't want me to get restricted, do you?"

"They'd never do that. You're their darling. You can do no wrong."

"It only seems that way to you because I don't keep trying to break the rules deliberately the way you do."

"You trying to tell me it's my own fault?"

"That last blowup you had with your father—well, you admit you left the door to the garage open when the bikes got stolen."

"I lost my key."

"But, Kyle, all I'm saying is he was mad for good reason."

"I just can't take getting yelled at for every little thing. How'd you like being wrong all the time?"

"I wouldn't. That's why I try to stay inside the rules."

"It's easy for you. All you have to do is get in before midnight and keep your room clean, for God's sake. My father has a book of rules as thick as a telephone directory. I don't even know half of them until I break them. The thing is, he hates me, Anne. He really hates my guts."

Seeing his pain, she put her arms around him and pulled his head down to her breast. "I'm sorry," she said. "I shouldn't have said anything." He was all tensed up again. "I'm on your side, Kyle. I think you're a wonderful, fabulous person."

"Keep telling me that."

"You're wonderful, sweet, sensitive, deep, generous, loving—"

"That's me, all right. Generous, loving—do you love me?"

"Ummm, a little."

"Just a little, huh?"

"Ummm. Maybe a lot."

"I'm all right, then. You wouldn't just go around loving anybody. Not you." He sat up and looked at her, boyish, as he said, "Now I'm going to say something I've never said to any other girl."

She squinted at him. He looked serious. Serious declarations from Kyle Youngman? Her heart did a tricky beat as she realized she didn't want him to go further. Not now. She was only sixteen. She sat up and put her hand over his mouth.

He took her hand away. "What's the matter?"

"I'm not ready for you to say anything."

"But I need you, Anne. You've always been ready. You've been waiting for me half your life and you're mine. I love you."

And then his hands talked more tenderly than they ever had before, and they lay touching one another with whispery kisses and tangled lips and limbs while the red embers in the stove turned to ashes. Finally the chill drove them out of the tepee. He took her home.

The light shining through the closed curtains in the living room at one fifteen in the morning dimmed her elation. Someone in her family was waiting to give her a hard time for being late. Mother, probably. Now she was going to be smothered with guilt before she even set foot on the stairs.

She unlocked the door and stepped into the living room. All three of them were sitting there. Renee was still dressed in heels and a silk dress. Lily had been crying.

"What's the matter?" Anne asked, fearing disaster.

"You're what's the matter," Renee said. "I got in just a few minutes ago and found your mother worried sick about you and Grams here trying to console her."

"I'm sorry," Anne said. "We didn't notice what time it was until too late."

"How many times have you used that excuse?" Renee asked. "You promised your mother you'd be in on time. It's not right, Anne."

"It's hard to get in at midnight. Couldn't we make it later on Saturday night?"

"A girl your age should be in bed at midnight," Grams said. "Your mother is too easy with you as is."

"That's not true!"

"Well, you certainly don't listen to her anymore. And with that hooligan—"

"Kyle's not a hooligan."

"He has all the earmarks of one," Renee said. "Why can't he get you home on time?"

"Am I Cinderella? Do I have to watch the clock? Tonight we were way out in the country. My watch stopped."

"Way out in the country," Lily said. "Anne, can't you at least find out where you're going beforehand and leave a telephone number for me to call? I was frantic thinking that if something had happened to you, I wouldn't even know where to start looking for you."

"What were you doing out in the country?" Renee asked.

"Are you the prosecuting attorney, Renee?"

"Don't be fresh to your aunt," Grams answered. "What's become of you? You're acting like a trashy girl. Don't you care that you upset your mother?"

"Yes, I care." Anne's stomach clenched with familiar rage, but she forced herself to say calmly, "I'm sorry, as I said before, and next time—"

"There isn't going to be a next time," Grams said. "Your mother's had enough. You're to stop seeing that boy."

"No!"

"Mama!" Lily warned. She rubbed her eyes and explained to Anne, "You don't have to stop seeing him entirely, but once a week is all I'll allow."

"Mother, you've always trusted me. You've encouraged me

to think for myself and be independent. You can't all of a sudden start treating me like a baby."

"You see the way she talks to you?" Grams said to Lily. "I told you that fellow was a bad influence on her. She never used to talk back to you."

"That fellow," Anne said, "is the most wonderful boy I've ever met."

"He's the first," Grams said. "That's what makes him so wonderful."

"I think Grams is right," Renee said. "You're blind to Kyle's faults."

"What's so terrible about him?" Anne cried. "That he doesn't get places on time? That he puts his elbows on the table when he eats? That he doesn't like being grilled every time he sets foot in this house?"

"You're a different girl since you started going out with him," Grams said.

"How have I changed?"

"You're not as thoughtful," Renee said. "You've become self-centered, and I'm afraid—"

"I'm sixteen years old. Don't I have a right to be in love?"

"Oh, my God! She's in love," Grams said. "Now you see—I told you this would happen."

"Mama, please," Renee said. "Anne, you're still planning to go to college, aren't you?"

"Yes . . . I don't know . . . college is not the most important thing in my life. Maybe it was in yours, Renee, but I don't care that much about a career. I want to love and be loved. Mother," Anne begged, "*you* understand."

"I want you to begin seeing other boys besides him," Lily answered quietly. "One night a week with Kyle is enough. You need some basis of comparison."

"He's a troublemaker," Grams said.

"Mother!" Renee warned her.

"What trouble has he ever gotten into?" Anne demanded.

"Anne, don't use that tone to your grandmother," Lily said. "Stop treating us like the enemy. We're your family."

"You want me to stop seeing Kyle. I can't. I can't do that."

"All we want is for you to have the things in life we missed," Renee said.

"You can't make me live the kind of life you want for yourselves. I have to decide what I want for me."

"You're not mature enough to decide," Grams said. "You're just a child."

"I know I've always encouraged you to make your own decisions, Anne," her mother said, "but now, the way you're behaving—I'm so scared for you."

"Think what it would do to your mother if something happened to you." Renee said.

"I have a right to live too," Anne protested. "I have to make my own mistakes. You can't keep me wrapped in cotton wool so that nothing ever happens to me. I'm not a doll. Once a week won't work, Mother. I have to be with Kyle."

"She ought to be locked in her room until she comes to her senses," Grams said, grim-faced.

Renee smiled wryly. "You don't want her climbing out of the window, Mama. She might fall and break her leg."

"That'd be better than what else she'll break."

Lily closed her eyes, looking so wretched that Anne felt guilty. "Anne," Lily said. "I want you to promise me you'll see Kyle only once a week, and that you'll accept dates with other boys if they ask you out or go out with Dodie to places where you might meet others."

"Mother, please! It's not fair."

"I can't make it any fairer. What I'd really like is for you to stop seeing Kyle altogether for a while. You need a cooling-off period. Trust our judgment in this, darling," Lily said.

"But I don't. I can't," Anne said. "I hate what you're doing to me. You're taking advantage because I listen to you and I'm a good daughter."

"We love you. Please remember that." Lily's eyes brimmed. Anne turned on her heel and rushed up to her bedroom. What could she do? Tell Kyle she could only see him once a week? He'd be furious. "Who means more to you?" he'd ask. "You," she would say. "Then tell them you'll do as you please. They can't stop you. They're not going to tie you to your bed physically." She lay biting her knuckle, thinking, too agitated to get ready for bed.

9

Monday evening Anne completed her report for Human Ecology and trailed downstairs in search of company. The family was gathered in the living room. Renee was working on the *New York Times* crossword puzzle. Lily was frowning at a hem she was sewing under the poor light from Grams's Chinese lamp. Grams was staring out the window.

"You look like a lively bunch," Anne commented.

Lily looked up. "Finished with your homework, darling?"

"More or less." Anne sat down beside her mother, who hugged her. Anne hadn't held the ultimatum on Kyle against Lily, certain that Grams and Renee had pushed her into it. Grams still held fast to the old-fashioned restrictions by which she'd been raised almost seventy years ago. It was Grams whom Anne resented.

"Anybody besides me in the mood for a sundae tonight?" Renee asked.

"Are you willing to drive us all to the ice-cream parlor?" Lily asked.

"I'm not getting dressed to go out," Grams said. "My fingers ache too much."

"Poor Mama. Can I get you some aspirin?" Lily went to her mother and lifted Grams's gnarled hands to examine them.

"You ought to try that new doctor I found, Mama," Renee said. "Your Dr. Fleder's out of the Dark Ages."

"No doctor can do me any good. What I've got is old age and there's no sense wasting your hard-earned money on looking for a cure for that."

Renee frowned at her mother's hands and muttered about health insurance coverage. She said pain made her feel helpless, and she had seemed to suffer more visibly during Lily's mastectomy than Lily had.

Grams is lucky, Anne thought. If Lily had stayed married and Renee had started a family of her own, Grams would just be an extra burden instead of the hub of their lives. Funny that they didn't resent it. Devoted daughters, they behaved as if they enjoyed catering to Grams. Did they expect Anne to follow in their footsteps? Just thinking about it made her feel trapped. Maybe that was why they didn't like Kyle. He was a threat to them. They wanted her to go to college, but did they really want her to fall in love and get married and raise a family someday? Did they really, in their hearts, want her to leave them? She was so deep into her suspicions that she was startled when Renee invited her along to get the fixings for some sundaes.

"Sure," Anne said. She was glad of the opportunity to talk to Renee alone.

Anne wriggled into the soft blue velour upholstery of Renee's car thinking of how feminine the car was—white outside, pale blue inside. Renee kept it up as meticulously as she kept herself. She spent a lot of time on the appearance of things. Just what Kyle neglected. No wonder she didn't like him.

An old man in a big car shot across the intersection as the light changed. Renee avoided a collision with only a "tst" of annoyance.

"You're a good driver."

"Thank you, cookie. It's going to be fun giving you driving practice when you turn seventeen and finish your Driver's Ed class."

Anne nodded. She would have preferred being taught by her mother, but Lily was a miserable driver. She crept cautiously into traffic or whizzed across intersections against the lights as the old man had. She drove as if every minute on the road was a gamble.

"Renee, I'm angry at you about the other night," Anne began. "You really have no right to influence how my mother brings me up."

"I have a right to state my opinions," Renee said, and added with feeling, "You're not just my niece, you know—you're the daughter I never had."

"But I'm smothering in mothers. I hate being treated as if I don't have a mind of my own."

"No question you're an intelligent, sensible girl, Anne, but you lack what your mother and grandmother and I are loaded with—experience."

"You never had an experience that relates to Kyle and me, Renee."

"You'd be surprised."

"Here we go with secrets again," Anne said.

"All right. The time has come to tell you about my friend, but swear you'll never repeat this to Grams."

"He's a married man."

"Yes," Renee said matter-of-factly, "now, do you want to hear about it or not?"

Anne nodded dumbly. Despite her wild guess, she was shocked.

Renee turned into the park and stopped under a streetlight facing the pond. The naked trees trembled, raked by the wind under the blackened sky. It was quiet in the car except for the uneven tapping of the rain on the roof. Instead of looking at her, Renee stared out at the rain dimpling the dark water of the pond as she began. "I did what often happens. I fell in love with my boss. We started off as friends twelve years ago and then— He's married, as you guessed. By the time I realized he couldn't bring himself to leave his wife and children for me, I'd gotten too attached to him to break off the relationship. Most of the time I go out with 'a friend,' it's Avery I'm seeing."

"And his wife doesn't know?"

"Yes, she knows. She's told him she doesn't care so long as he supports her and keeps up appearances. She says it's for the children's sake."

"What about you?"

"If I wanted to see anyone else, Avery would encourage me. He knows it's unfair to me as things are. I wanted children, and now I'll never have any of my own. But he's the man I love, so I make the best of what I do have." Renee smiled. "Settling for what you can get, it's called."

"It sounds sort of—" Anne wanted to say "sordid," but she didn't want to hurt Renee's feelings. ". . . awkward."

"It's no picnic. People at work make remarks. That's why I have no friends there. I don't like the situation, believe me. It doesn't make me feel good about myself—quite the contrary, in fact."

"What's he like?"

"He's a kind, quiet man with a lot of emotional problems. He's fifteen years older than me and not what you'd call good-looking. But we share the same political and social interests. We both love the theater and travel. I know all about his children and I give him advice on their problems when he asks my opinion, which he does often. We're very close, Avery and I."

"Then it's not so bad? I mean, your life?" She didn't want to feel sorry for Renee too now—not her aunt who was the big success in the family.

"I do okay, Anne. I have a job I enjoy. I have you and your mother and Grams. I have part of Avery. That's not everything, but it keeps me going."

"I can't believe Grams doesn't know about him. Doesn't she even suspect?"

"No, and don't you give her any hints. She'd be horrified. She'd be after me to drop Avery, and I can't do that."

"That's just how I feel about Kyle," Anne pointed out.

"Which brings me to my reason for telling you all this," Renee said. "Believe me, if it's wrong from the beginning, it's not going to get better. Kyle's not the boy for you. Stop now before he hurts you."

They sat there in silence until Renee asked, "Didn't you hear me?"

"Renee, why didn't you ever leave Grams and get your own place?"

"Primarily because she needs me. When my father died, I'd just gotten my first job. His insurance wasn't enough for Grams to live on for long, and she was too old to find a suitable job and too young for social security. I've always gotten along fine with her, so I stayed. Besides, it's nice to have somebody to come home to at night. I'm a very family-oriented person. I guess companionship means more to me than independence."

"Well," Anne said. "There it is. You and I are not the same, Renee. You don't understand my needs."

With a sigh Renee released the hand brake and began backing up to continue on their way to the ice-cream parlor. "All right, I won't say another word, but think about what I said, at least. If you ruin your life, it'll kill us all."

Ridiculous to compare Renee's miserable situation to hers with Kyle, Anne thought. Kyle wasn't married and he loved her and only her, even if the family couldn't believe that. They were unreasonable. She'd just have to stop listening to them and take charge of her own life.

As soon as Dodie stepped out of the cab that she'd had to take from the train station, Anne grabbed her and hugged her. "I'm so glad you're back, Dodie."

"What a welcome! And I was only gone a few days. Lend me two dollars to pay the driver. I'm short," Dodie said.

Anne got her purse and handed over her lunch money. Dodie paid the cab driver and waved him off. "Anne, you should have been there. I was a smash hit—or anyway my costumes were. Everybody says I should definitely go in for costume design—even the male lead, who hates my guts. I took pictures. I hope they come out." She walked into the living room. "Hi, Grams. How you feeling?" She kissed Grams warmly as if she were indeed part of the family.

"We missed you," Grams said without taking her eyes from her afternoon soap opera. "It was so quiet in the house."

"Well, now I'm back, we'll liven the place up. But first"—Dodie sprawled on the couch—"I'm going to have to sleep for a week. I haven't had any sleep since I left. It was party, party,

party and talking all the time. Anne, you look sad. What's the matter?"

"I'll help you unpack," Anne said.

"What's happened?" Dodie asked as soon as they were alone upstairs.

"Kyle came for dinner Friday night."

"So?"

"So that didn't improve anything. And I got in late again Saturday night, and Mother says I can only see Kyle one night a week from now on."

"You're kidding!"

"I know he's going to give me a hard time about it. How am I going to tell him, Dodie?"

"Well, now let's see," Dodie said. "You could give it to him straight and hope he'll just grumble and get used to it—unless you're scared he'll fill the time up with other girls."

"Kyle would never do that," Anne said.

"Oh, wouldn't he? Face it, kid. Kyle's fooled around with every decent-looking girl in the high school."

"But he loves me."

"Yeah, but you're asking for trouble if you set him loose," Dodie said.

Anne was annoyed. "I thought you liked Kyle."

"I do. I'm thinking of stealing him away from you soon as I lose thirty pounds and turn gorgeous."

Anne sat down and began gnawing on her knuckle, disturbed by Dodie's image of Kyle.

"You have another option," Dodie said. "You could sneak out. Tell your family you're going someplace with me and meet him instead. Kids do that all the time."

"I wouldn't."

"Well, if you're going to stand on principles— Okay. You could also—now think before you reject this one—you could tell your mother you're going to see Kyle whether she likes it or not—like civil disobedience. You might get away with it. They're not going to hold you here by force."

Anne nodded.

"Well . . . would you do it?" Dodie asked.

"I'm not sure I could. It would upset them, and I don't want to cause Mother any more grief," Anne said.

"You're too good for your own good."

"I'm not good at all. Dodie, I don't know what to do. What would you do?"

"Me? Simple. I'd sneak out and see Kyle."

Anne considered but couldn't decide. "Anyway," she said, "there's a party Saturday night. We're all three invited."

"He'll expect to see you Friday, too."

"Friday he has to work at the garage," Anne said.

"Good. That leaves Sunday as your only problem. Maybe you can get sick for Sunday."

"I'm not going to sneak behind *his* back either. I guess I've got to tell him the truth."

"Good luck," Dodie said, and her tone indicated Anne would need it.

Anne called Kyle that night, at his house, which she rarely did. To her dismay, his father answered. She mumbled her name and he barked, "Kyle!" Just that short sound had so much venom in it that she winced.

"Are you in trouble again?" she asked when Kyle answered.

"No more than usual. Dad's ticked off about something that happened at work. How come you're calling? Your house on fire or something?"

"Not that bad. It's Mother. She's laid down the law."

"You gotta be in by midnight, huh?"

"Besides that."

"Okay, spill it. I can't stand drawn-out executions. She doesn't want you seeing me anymore."

"Once a week is all. They're mad because we kept getting home so late."

"Don't give me that. They don't want you seeing me. God, those women all hate me—even your mother. You'd think I had a jail record or something."

"Kyle, once a week isn't so bad."

"Yeah? Listen, Anne. They'll keep putting up roadblocks until they break us up. You're going to have to make up your mind. It's either them or me."

"You're mad at me."

"Sure I am. I'd never have started up with you if I'd known you were such a mama's girl."

"I knew you were going to make it impossible for me. Kyle, please, let's wait until the weekend. Maybe something will change by then."

"The only thing that can change is you. I've already tried coming for dinner."

"Say you love me," she begged when Kyle's father yelled for him to get off the phone.

"Love you," Kyle said, and hung up.

That evening she tried talking her mother into relenting, but Lily stood firm. "It's for your own good, darling," she said.

I'm going to lose him, Anne thought. One way or another, I'm starting to lose him already.

"Dodie!" Anne yelled when she finally saw Kyle zooming into the driveway to pick them up for the party Saturday evening. Instead of honking, he came to the door, which she opened just as he was about to ring the bell. He pressed his extended finger against her chin instead and kissed her.

"How's my babe?" He was in shirt sleeves, although it felt like snow.

"Fine," Anne said. "I think Dodie's almost ready. Come in and sit down for a minute."

"Is the dragon lady waiting for me?"

"Grams isn't feeling well. She's in bed."

"Ah, too bad! I'm fired up to match her blast for blast tonight. Where's your mom?" Kyle asked.

"She and Renee went to an early movie."

"Then what do we need to go to the party for? We could stay here and make out on the couch."

"Funny," she said.

"I've been thinking about us, babes." His voice was deep and serious.

She looked at him wide-eyed as he put his hands on her shoulders and fixed her eyes with his. "I think you may be my one true lady."

"Kyle!"

"Hey-hey-hey!" Dodie bellowed. "You're missing my grand entrance. How about turning around, you two?" She was coming down the stairs costumed in an asymmetrical white cape trimmed with a spiral of red.

"What are you dressed up as, Dodie, a fat candy cane?" Kyle asked.

Dodie froze midstaircase and stared at him openmouthed. "You big ape!" she yelled finally. "This is a costume I designed for that musical. Everybody said it's a knockout."

"Yeah, but Halloween's over."

"Anne, tell him to quit stepping all over my feelings," Dodie said.

"Dodie, you look—spectacular," Anne said diplomatically. "But maybe an ordinary dress would be better tonight. I mean, people won't know what to make of anything so fancy."

"You're telling me I look like a clown, huh? So what. That's what I usually come on as." She stomped back upstairs.

"We hurt her feelings," Anne said.

"Me and my big mouth!" Kyle said. "You'd better go after her. I'll wait in the car."

Dodie was standing in front of the walk-in closet surveying her wardrobe. The costume lay in a heap on the floor. "What should I wear, then?" Dodie asked.

"You mad?"

"Sure I'm mad. The big ape! He sure is no master of tact. And neither are you. How about this tent dress? I have beads that look good with it."

"Fine, Dodie." Anne kissed her cheek. "I'm sorry. You know I think you're wonderful."

"Well, you're right. I am wonderful, and a fantastic dresser besides." Dodie wore the tent dress with a belt. She was proud that she could buckle the belt, but Anne was wary of complimenting her on that. Dodie had lost a lot of weight. Grams was worried about her loss of appetite and wanted to send her to a doctor to see if she was healthy. Renee had told Grams to leave Dodie alone. Renee kept telling Dodie how much better she looked, which Dodie privately told Anne only made her realize how awful she'd looked to Renee before.

Downstairs they joined Kyle, who was leaning against his car.

"Well, charm boy, do I pass inspection now?" Dodie asked him.

"Now you could pose for a fashion ad." He grinned at her.

"Thanks." She struggled into her winter jacket.

"You know, for queen-size ladies," Kyle added.

Dodie tried to hit him, but he hugged her, pinioning her

arm, and kissed her cheek, saying, "Hey, good-looking, want to join my harem? I could use an armful like you."

"Big shot!" Dodie said. "You can't even manage the woman you've got."

"Oh, I don't know about that," Anne said, slipping under the other arm, which Kyle held out to her. They exchanged a kiss, proper as sipping tea, but Anne caught Dodie's expression. Jealous. For Dodie's sake, Anne would have to avoid physical contact with Kyle around her.

Kyle watched Dodie squeezing into the backseat of his car with a critical eye. "Hey, Dodie," he said. "No kidding now. You're losing weight. It looks good."

"Can I say thanks? You going to put me down?"

"You're a cute kid. I mean it," he said, and slid into the driver's seat.

"You're in such a good mood tonight," Anne commented to him.

"Things are beginning to go my way. I can work Friday nights steady at the garage if I want—no more filling in—and some guy I forgot I loaned money to showed up and paid me back. Can you believe it? Now, if we could only plan a campaign to win over the dragon lady and her daughters, I'll be in really good shape. What do you say, Dodie? What would make them like me?"

"You could get into Harvard."

"Besides that."

"You could stop spitting chewing tobacco all over their floors."

"Oh, come on. There's got to be an easier way than that. I know they don't think I'm good enough for Anne. Truth is, I'm probably not."

"You're wonderful for me," Anne said.

"So how am I going to win them over?"

"How about a five-pound box of chocolates?"

"But *you* already like me, Dodie."

"That's true. Maybe you can't make them like you," Dodie said. "Did you ever think of that?"

"That leaves it up to Anne, then," Kyle said with a meaningful glance at her.

"Please, Kyle," she said faintly.

"Okay. Forget it," he said. "Tonight we just relax and have fun."

They walked into the tiled recreation room where the stereo was already filling the air with pulsing music and kids were clumped in still lifes here and there. "Hi, everybody, Dodie's here!" Dodie yelled at the top of her lungs.

"Oh, my God! Here comes Big Mama," one boy said.

"Listen to that beat!" Dodie said. She concentrated on absorbing rhythm into her body, standing all alone and dancing with most of the eyes in the room on her. There was applause and an offer of partners. With the next number the party got under way, as if her entrance had signaled its beginning.

"Isn't she amazing?" Anne said to Kyle.

"I'll have to admit she's not the problem I thought she was going to be. I like her."

"She likes you too," Anne said, and meant more than as just a friend.

"I know," he said. Anne wondered if he did.

Kyle led Anne onto the dance floor. Like Dodie, he seemed to ingest the music, and his body became a visual expression of the sound. Anne moved self-consciously, wishing she could just let go and enjoy herself the way Kyle and Dodie could. When the music took on a faster beat, Anne quit dancing. She shook her head at Kyle and backed off the dance floor. He shrugged, not letting go of the rhythm, and looked around.

Finding Dodie still out there, he joined her. They rippled and jiggled and wriggled and kicked, moved in synchronized motions that had people standing in a circle clapping them on. Anne watched, proud of them both.

"Is he a good lover?" Dodie asked her when they were home in bed that night.

"Um hum."

"Rough or gentle?"

"Sometimes one, sometimes the other," Anne said.

"And you like it?"

"As much as you like dancing."

"And you look like you don't have anything below your waist," Dodie said. "You look so cool. I can't believe you."

"Have you ever made love, Dodie?"

"I think I'd be scared," Dodie answered.

"Oh, Dodie!"

"Well, weren't you the first time?"

Anne thought back. She remembered him saying, "Are you sure you're sure?" and she had answered, "Yes, I'm sure." She laughed. "It's the only part of me that isn't repressed," Anne told Dodie now.

"It may be the only part of me that is," Dodie said.

"You and Kyle looked terrific on the dance floor."

"Thanks. Boy, that's two compliments in one night. I'm really living." She was quiet for a while and Anne thought she'd fallen asleep. Then softly in the dark Dodie said, "I really like him a lot, Anne."

"Dodie, I love you, but he's mine."

"I know."

Anne smiled to herself. Her sister-friend! She hoped for Dodie's sake the crush she had on Kyle wasn't too serious.

Dodie had so much to offer. She deserved a guy of her own, not the dim reflection of another's relationship. Dodie! Loving her, Anne wanted all kinds of happiness for her—all except the special bit that belonged to Anne alone.

10

Sunday morning the phone rang when they were all slouching around the kitchen getting themselves breakfast, still in robes —or, in Dodie's case, a frilly nightgown. Dodie was making pancakes for Lily. Renee was waiting for her turn at the toaster. Anne raced for the phone.

"Hi," Kyle said. "I'm in the hospital."

"The hospital? What happened?"

"It's a long story. You coming?"

"Sure I'm coming."

"Good. I gotta get off this phone. Not supposed to be using it. Room four fourteen. Don't stop at the desk. Just come straight up."

She set the receiver back and stood there trying to process what he'd told her. In the kitchen she heard Grams say, "Who's calling at this hour?"

"It's after nine, Mama."

"But it's Sunday morning."

"If we weren't going to Williamstown, I'd sleep until noon," Lily said.

"You'll love the museum, Dodie," Renee said. "It has one of the finest collections of French Impressionists I've seen."

"Anything's fun when you do it all together as a family," Dodie said.

Good thing that Dodie craved family, Anne thought. Today she would have to substitute as daughter in this one. Dodie wouldn't mind, but the rest of them would. According to the once-a-week rule, last night's date with Kyle should be it for the weekend. Well, she couldn't help it. This was an emergency. She walked into the kitchen and said, "I'm sorry, but you'll all have to go without me. That was Kyle. He's in the hospital."

"What happened?" Renee asked.

"I don't know, but he wants me there."

"How do you know he was really calling from the hospital?" Renee asked.

"Renee!" Anne said and turned her back on her aunt.

"Didn't he tell you *anything?*" Dodie asked.

"He said he couldn't talk. He just gave his room number."

"They won't even let her upstairs until visiting hours," Grams said.

"It's odd that he didn't say what was wrong," Lily said. "Maybe you should call him back and find out, Anne."

"Mother! Kyle's in the *hospital.* Doesn't anyone care? He's hurt. He needs me and I'm going to him now." She couldn't believe that they were so unfeeling. She ran upstairs and began dressing. She was brushing her hair when the door opened and Lily and Dodie trooped in.

"Renee had a good idea," Lily said. "Suppose we all go to the hospital with you, and you go up and see Kyle—if they let you—and then come to Williamstown with us after. He can't be in bad shape if he could use the phone."

"I'm going to be at the hospital all day."

"No, darling. I'm sure they won't let you stay. You're not his wife or his mother. The most you'll be allowed to see him for is an hour or so. Remember the rules when I was in the hospital?"

Anne shook her head. "Really, I'm sorry, but he's—he comes first right now. I'll see you all tonight."

On her way out of the house she heard Renee on the phone. She stopped long enough to hear Renee ask, "Do you have a Kyle Youngman? Just admitted last night or this morning?" Anger swept through Anne. They were checking to see if the whole thing was a trick to get around the once-a-weekend restriction. She was about to tell Renee how nasty she thought her suspicions were when she heard her aunt ask, "Could you tell me just how ill he is? . . . Well, can he have visitors? . . . I see. Thank you." Renee clicked the receiver down and called over her shoulder, "Anne, you can't see him until one."

"I don't care," Anne said stubbornly. "I'm going now." She slammed out the front door, got her bike out of the garage, and headed toward the hospital. It was cold. The sky was a uniform gray, laced shut at the edges by brown tree branches. An oak shook its dead leaves at her. She sped through residential streets and along the main road past the shopping area, barely noticing what she was passing. Kyle had sounded so bleak on the phone. What could have happened to him between last night and this morning? A car accident on the way home? She locked her bike into the rack near the side door of the hospital. "Come straight up," he had said.

She took the first staircase and started climbing, her heart racing, nervous that she might be stopped and sent back. She didn't like ignoring rules, but this was for Kyle. In the corridor on the fourth floor she checked room numbers. Luckily she found four fourteen without passing a nurses' station or seeing anyone.

Kyle was in the bed near the window. The bed near the door was made up but empty. Anne halted in the doorway, shocked by the sight of him. His left side, including his arm and shoulder, was covered with bandages. Two young nurses were sitting on either side of his bed. He was grinning. That took the heat out of Anne's sympathy. It didn't look as if he needed her quite so desperately as she had thought.

"So you're the dummy, huh?" Kyle was asking one girl.

"Right. I have to study all the time just to squeak by. Hee Chung here aces every test and never studies at all."

"That's not true. I study," said the petite Korean girl with childish arms and a sweet face.

"But anyway, I give the best back rubs," the other assured him.

"You going to come by and show me when I get these bandages off?"

"Can I trust you when you have the use of both arms? Right now I can probably take you, but two arms—" the nurse teased.

"You can't even take me with one. Come on this side of the bed and let's arm-wrestle," Kyle said.

"I thought you were sick," Anne said from the door.

"Anne! You got here." Kyle's grin spread and he held out the good arm to her.

She went to his side and kissed his cheek, saying, "I thought you were miserable, and here you are surrounded by pretty women."

"That's because he's already famous in the hospital," the

one nurse said. "Nobody could get over how he kept joking the whole time they dug the glass out of his arm."

"I must have been in shock," Kyle said.

"No, you're a very brave boy," Hee Chung told him.

"Nice girls," Kyle said after the two nurses had left.

"You're terrible. You didn't need me at all, and now the whole family's mad at me for not going with them to Williamstown."

"I do need you, babes. I was just shooting the bull with those girls, just passing the time until you got here." He brought her hand to his lips and kissed it.

"Tell me what happened."

"I was hit by a drunk driver going around that circle on River Road. Turned the car over trying to avoid smashing headfirst into a tree and smashed my arm through the window instead."

"Oh, Kyle!"

"Wait. That's not the part that shook me. Guy comes by and sees me lying there; so they call an ambulance and I'm in the emergency room at three o'clock in the morning getting the glass picked out of me. So my dad walks in, and you know what the first thing he says to me is? 'I warned you not to drive when you're drunk.' First words out of his mouth, so help me. I'm lying there on the table, and he's so sure it's my own fault he doesn't even wait to hear what happened."

"But you explained to him, didn't you?"

"Why should I explain? I said, 'Yeah, Dad, you got it.' So he starts ranting on about what a no-good bum I am right there in the emergency room until the doctor finally told him to wait outside. My father still doesn't know what happened."

"Is the arm very damaged?"

"Messy-looking. I'll have some first-class scars—no damage to the muscles, though. I've got a couple of cracked ribs too, but that's nothing. I thought I was gonna be dead when that guy plowed into me. Believe me, I got off easy."

She kissed his eyelids, which were half closed. "What a terrible end to a lovely evening. If only you hadn't taken the long way home!"

"I didn't exactly go home after I dropped you off, Annie. I stopped in at a bar to see some guys I know and had a couple of beers. I wasn't drunk. Not even slightly. Don't start thinking like my father."

"I'm not, Kyle."

"I couldn't stand to have you lose faith in me too. Listen, I made up my mind. I'm not going home when I get out of here. I'm going to take off. No sense waiting through this year. I'll never make it. I'll either explode and hit him or he'll convince me I really am rotten. I'm heading west—Arizona maybe. The desert sounds good to me. I can get a job fixing cars or doing construction or something. No more crap from my father or teachers or anybody."

"You won't even have a high school diploma then."

"I can get one or take an equivalency exam. Senior year is a farce anyway. We've already learned all the stuff that counts."

"But if you leave now, how will you— Are you just going to give up on the idea of college?"

"Anne, do you really think college is for me?"

"You're smart. When you want to, you can get grades as good as anybody's," she said.

"But how am I gonna sit still in a classroom for four more years? I hate sitting there listening to some teacher talk at me like he's God's right hand. I hate being told to do this, do that. Here's a test—let's see you fail. And picky little rules just to make you squirm. The older I get, the harder it is for me to knuckle under."

"Kyle, you're all worked up, and probably in a lot of pain. You can't think clearly now."

"I can take that kind of pain," Kyle said.

"What about your mother?"

"She won't care. After I'm gone, he can stomp around yelling, and she'll just duck. She'll be glad it's so peaceful without me around to fight him. Besides, she has the twins. They're good kids. I'm the only troublemaker in the family."

"I don't want you to leave," Anne said in a choked voice.

"Listen, babes. I've been ready for this for a long time. I saved up some money to get me started. I've just been waiting for a shove."

"But why so far away? Couldn't you move out of the house and get a job here in town? You could live with a friend and finish high school at least."

"I want a clean break."

"With me too?"

"Hey, Annie! I'm not going forever. I'll come back to claim you when you're all grown up and ready for me."

"Once you leave, you won't come back for me. You'll be too different."

"And will you stay the same?"

"About you I will."

"You'll always be my girl?"

"I told you not to say you loved me unless you meant it," she said.

"I do mean it." He picked up her hand again. "How come you're so cold?"

"Because," she said, using all her control to hold back the tears.

He blew gently into her palm and laid it against his cheek and closed his eyes. "You could come with me when I leave."

Her mind squeezed shut on the possibility. Mom, she

thought. And Grams's fury. Renee's disappointment. And Dodie. She'd lose them all if she went with Kyle. All the people who loved her in the balance with him. Choose. Choose either but not both. The impossibility of it overwhelmed her.

"Think about it," he said. "You'd be my old lady. We might jump around a lot and you'd have to work too. There wouldn't be much in it for you until I make it big."

"Except you."

"Question is, am I enough for you? I mean, when the chips are down, do you really love me, Annie?"

His eyes bored into her as if he wanted to see the answer deep inside her head, but he couldn't see what she didn't know yet. A gray-haired nurse squeaked by on rubber soles, glanced into the room, and firmly announced the visiting hours.

"Just another few minutes," Kyle begged. "Please. This is important."

"Five minutes and that's it. We're not supposed to have visitors on the floor now."

"Thanks." Kyle flashed her his winner's smile. "Thanks a lot."

"I love you enough," Anne said. Tears slid over her eyelids and down her cheeks. She shivered.

"You better think about it. Give it a few days. I don't want you to come and be regretting it half the time. That would just drag me down," he said.

"But you do want me with you?"

"Yeah, I want you. Sure, I want you."

She kissed him fiercely, brushed his hair with her fingers. "I'll be back when it's visiting hours," she told him. Then she ran down the same staircase she'd used coming up. It was eleven. Visiting hours began at one. That gave her two hours to sit alone and think. She found a niche in the lobby facing a window that looked out on the street. She stared at the passing traffic, watched an old woman walking a fat muffin of a dog. His old lady, he had said. No dream she'd ever had had been so frightening. But if she really loved him, she would put him first. If she really loved him, she would be willing to sacrifice anything for him, even her family.

It would be dreary a lot of the time. What kind of job could she get without a high school diploma? Could she be a waitress? Work in a factory? Maybe she could earn money babysitting or be a homemaker for some woman who worked. It could be a challenge. She'd learn a lot with Kyle. How to run a household. She could do that probably. At least she knew how to cook and clean. And college? She could manage that someday. Only Lily—she couldn't, she just couldn't do this to her mother. Hadn't Lily said, "You're all I have?" Of course, Lily had Grams and Renee, so she wasn't entirely alone while Kyle had no one but her.

By the time Anne returned to Kyle's room, she was so tense that it was a relief to find his parents sitting there. In their presence the conversation was confined to Kyle's injury, how the accident had really happened, and who his mother should call to cover Kyle's various commitments.

At two thirty a boy Kyle knew who worked as an orderly at the hospital came to visit. More polite conversation. Visiting hours ended and Anne hadn't had another chance to speak to Kyle alone. "I'll come after school tomorrow," she promised him.

"Yeah. Tell the kids I need visitors," he said.

She raised a questioning eyebrow. Didn't he want to be alone with her? Then she realized that, of course, the decision was hers. He wasn't about to talk her into it. And if she went with him, they'd have plenty of time alone with each other.

Her stomach was clenched so tight when she got home that she couldn't eat supper and barely heard their report of the good time they'd had in Williamstown.

"How is he?" Dodie asked her.

"He's okay," Anne said, and that was all.

A cold drizzle had shut the world down early that Sunday evening—dark out at five. Waspish weather made the lamplit warmth inside the house seem especially cozy. They were gathered in the living room, where Dodie was parodying the high-kicking dancers on a TV variety show. Renee and Lily were laughing at Dodie while Grams complained that she couldn't pay attention to the show with Dodie cutting up all over the place. Anne was there with them and yet not there. Inside her head she and Kyle were riding galloping horses across a golden slab of desert toward a backdrop of solid blue sky—Arizona. The more she thought about it, the more she wanted to go. It would be the greatest adventure of her life—the first, the only adventure. Her life was regulated by obligation and affection. She was so tired of tameness. For once she would be wild.

"Tell me what went on in the hospital today," Dodie said when they were getting ready for bed that night.

"Nothing. He'll be all right."

"Something happened. You've been sleepwalking all evening."

"I'm sorry I left you alone with the family all day," Anne said. "Were you mad at me?"

"Why should I be? Your family's the best audience! I even made Grams laugh. Can you believe it? She wouldn't look at any nude pictures in the museum. She stuck her chin out and walked right by those gorgeous Renoirs without looking. But

Renee knows a lot about art and she's good company. And your mother is a sweetie pie. Did you know that Grams and Renee are worried about her because she poops out so fast? I thought you said she was cured of the cancer?"

"She's supposed to be. They say if you survive five years—But it hasn't been five years yet."

"It must have been horrible, huh?"

"Well, it came right after the divorce and her big business failure when she had that antiques shop. And the operation is horrible, especially for a woman like my mother. She was always the pretty one. Renee was smart and Mother was pretty. Now she feels disfigured. Well, she is, but I mean, she can't accept that she still looks fine on the outside. After the operation was when she put on all the weight and kind of retreated into the family." Talking about it brought back some of the sorrow. Pity for her mother would trap her, Anne knew. She didn't want to think about it now. The next thing Dodie said made it even worse.

"They were really upset that you went to Kyle today. Grams was furious with you. You should have heard her . . . I like Grams. She's such a tough old bird. You can fight with her where your mother's too easy to hurt. It's good you're so sensitive."

"I'm not sensitive enough. . . . Dodie, I may do a terrible thing."

"Such as?" Dodie's bed creaked as she raised herself on one elbow and looked toward Anne.

"This is top secret," Anne said. "You can't tell anyone—not anyone."

"I *knew* something was going on. I could tell just by looking at you. Listen, what's a best friend for if not to keep your secrets? Tell me."

"Kyle's leaving town as soon as he's well enough to go. He wants me to go with him."

"And you're *going?*" Dodie asked.

"I want to."

"Anne, *you?* I can't believe it! I'd never have imagined in a million years that you'd— Really? You'd run away with him?"

"Wouldn't you?"

"Me? Sure. Why not? I have nothing to lose," Dodie said. "Larry might worry, but my mother would be—I don't know, annoyed or angry. It wouldn't hurt her the way—" She stopped and Anne said it for her.

"The way my mother would be hurt."

"You're in some bind, aren't you? And you're going to run away with him?"

"Do you think it would kill her?"

"She's got Grams and Renee. She'd survive. Boy, that would be something. You've always been such a goody-goody."

"I'm not seventeen years old yet," Anne said. "I'm too young to be an old woman."

"Yeah, I don't blame you. If he asked me to go with him, I'd be off in a minute."

But that was not what Anne wanted to hear. Carefully she asked, "If you were *me,* would you go with Kyle? I mean me with my mother to consider?"

Dodie didn't answer. So much time passed that Anne thought she wasn't going to answer. Then Dodie said in a guarded voice, "You're not pregnant, are you?"

"Of course not."

"Then I think running away with Kyle is probably the dumbest thing you could do to yourself."

"Why?" Anne argued. "It's selfish for me to go, but doesn't everybody have a right to be selfish when they're in love? I don't want to end up like Renee or like Mother. And how do I know I'll ever love anyone else as much as Kyle? I can't take a chance on missing out on the most important thing in my life, can I?"

"And what about college? You're an honor student."

"Kyle comes first."

"You're too young."

"Only in years, not inside me," Anne said. "Dodie, would you stay on here with the family until Christmas if I go? Would you stay and sort of fill in for me?"

"Nobody can fill in for you. Don't kid yourself," Dodie said.

"I'm letting you down too, aren't I?"

"What gets me is the idea of you dropping out of school. That's like throwing half your future out the window."

"Well, he'll be in the hospital for a while yet. I have time to think it over," Anne said.

"Yeah. Think hard. And I thought *I* was the romantic one!" Dodie said.

11

Anne knew Kyle's room would be jammed with visitors after school, and she wanted to tell him her decision in private. Luckily she had a study hall last period. To cut it, all she had to do was have someone sign her name on the attendance sheet for her. Still, she felt bold having done it.

She walked by the nurses' station, where a fading bouquet of chrysanthemums decorated the counter and a nurse flipped cards in plastic covers. An emaciated young man shuffled down the corridor pushing a metal IV holder. He eyed Anne with interest, and she looked away. Kyle's room was empty.

"He's probably down in the lounge," the young man said.

"Thanks." Anne smiled at him politely and walked to the end of the hall, where a small area was fitted with plastic and chrome armchairs and a TV set. Kyle was sprawled there, legs out and head resting on the back of the only couch. He was throwing rubber darts at a venereal disease poster. Dodie was sitting cross-legged on the floor at his feet.

"Dodie! How come you're here so early?" Anne asked in dismay.

"Hey, babes, come put your arms around me and tell me that you love me," Kyle said in a woeful voice.

She was happy to oblige. "How are you feeling?" she asked him.

"Not too hot. This place gives me the creeps. Too many sick people."

"Will you be out soon?"

"Couple more days maybe."

"They're going to kick him out if he doesn't start behaving," Dodie said.

"Don't believe it. They love me."

"The head nurse calls his room the 'Social Center,' " Dodie said.

"Not my fault. Just my natural magnetism at work."

"Have you been here long?" Anne asked Dodie, and then, "Don't you have an eighth-period class today?"

"I took the afternoon off."

"She's giving me the business," Kyle complained. "Says you're a delicate flower that I'll crush if I drag you off to Arizona with me."

"Dodie! You traitor!"

"No way," Dodie said. "It's just the more I thought about what you told me, the more scared I got. Maybe you can't see what a disaster it would be, Anne, but Mr. Magnetism here sure should be able to get the picture."

"You came here to tell Kyle not to take me with him?" Anne was incredulous.

"You can't go with him," Dodie said firmly. "It would be wrong for you, wrong for your family, and wrong for him, too, in the long run."

"Dodie's a real know-it-all," Kyle said. His eyes were sulky. A stubble of light brown beard made him look dissolute.

"How could you?" Anne asked her. "I confided in you because you're my closest friend. I never would have if I'd thought you'd start running my life for me too."

"Who else is going to? You're not talking it over with your family before you take off, are you?"

"I trusted you."

"Right. I'm your best friend, and I'm telling you flat out. You need a college education more than you need Kyle."

"I'm not going to argue," Anne said icily. "Just don't ever do a thing like this again."

"Then who's going to protect you from yourself?" Dodie stood up. "All right. I'll leave you two alone. But you think about it. And, Kyle, it'll be on your conscience."

"Oh, my God, I can't believe this!" Anne said as Dodie flounced out. "She's so melodramatic. I'm sorry she bothered you, Kyle. I should never have told her anything."

"Take it easy, babes." He took her hand in his good one and pulled her so that her head rested on his shoulder and he could stroke the softness of her cheek and neck. "You're going with me, huh?"

"Yes."

"Made up your mind?"

"Yes."

"Love me?" She kissed him for answer.

"But suppose Dodie's right," Kyle said. "Before I strike it rich, there's likely to be some hard times. You're not built for sleeping in barns, working at crummy jobs, maybe going hungry and dirty sometimes. You're a handle-with-care kind of girl."

"No, I'm not—just untested."

"And that scholarship you could probably get that you'll be

giving up? Five years from now you going to hate me for what you missed?"

"Don't let Dodie get to you, Kyle. Her problem is, she's in love with you too."

"Oh, yeah?"

"No, that's not fair," Anne said. "She did think she was doing it for me, but she does have a crush on you. She took off all that weight because of you. You're the only one she's ever lost weight for."

"Well, she's a nice kid. Not my type, though."

For an instant Anne felt sorry for Dodie, then anger at her returned. A friend who wouldn't keep your confidences was no friend at all.

"By Thanksgiving I should have the car back," Kyle said. "Friends of mine in the garage are working on it, and my arm should be okay. If I don't get kicked out of the house before, we'll leave then."

That night when they were alone in the bedroom, Dodie told Anne, "I'm going to have to tell your family next."

"You do *that*, and I'll never forgive you. Never."

"I will, unless you tell them yourself," Dodie said coolly.

"You have no right. What kind of friend are you?"

"Your best friend. Anne, even if you hate me for it, I'll tell them if you don't."

"You tell them, and you can pack and go somewhere else. I won't want you here anymore." Dodie knew she meant it. Her eyes as she stared at Anne were solemn. It was hard in that small room to avoid each other, but they managed. Only Dodie fell asleep; Anne couldn't. She kept going over and over the arguments for and against her going, but whether she landed on should or shouldn't, her decision didn't change.

Dodie was as good as her word. The next evening when Anne came home from her after-school hospital visit, she found Grams and Renee in conference in the kitchen.

"I'm sorry I'm late," Anne said. "Oh, good. Nobody's set the table yet." She began laying out the straw place mats, aware that they were staring at her.

"Dodie told us something that can't be true," Grams said.

Anne clutched the silverware she had just removed from the drawer and asked, with her back toward them, "What did she tell you?"

"You're planning to run off with that fellow. You're running away from home with him."

"I'm not running away from home, Grams. I'm going with Kyle because I love him and want to be where he is."

"What about where we are? Don't we count for anything?" Grams asked.

"Of course you do. You're my family. I love you too, but it's not the same thing," Anne said.

"Ridiculous. You're sixteen years old, a baby. I never heard such silliness."

"I'm almost seventeen."

"Did he ask you to marry him?" Grams asked.

"No."

"He doesn't even think enough of you to ask you to marry him and you're running away with him?" Grams sounded outraged. "Don't you have any self-respect?"

"We never talked about marriage," Anne said.

"And rightly so," Renee said, butting in. "She's much too young."

"Renee, be quiet," Grams said.

"But you don't want her to marry him," Renee said.

"Let her ask him."

"You think he'll refuse me, Grams? Okay, I'll ask him."

"Anne," Renee began, "I can't believe you'd jeopardize your whole future like this. Do you want to be married at sixteen and pregnant while other girls go off to college? Hauling diapers to a Laundromat when you could be setting yourself up for a successful future?"

"I want to be loved. That's what I want."

"You are loved," Renee said.

"You love me because I'm the only child left in this family. But Kyle could love anyone, and he chose me."

"Ridiculous," Grams said again. "You'll have lots of young men after you."

"I don't want young men after me. I want Kyle."

"And your mother? You'd do this to your mother after all she's suffered?" Grams asked.

"Am I supposed to stay home and take care of my mother the rest of my life?"

"Listen to her!"

"Grams, if I were twenty-one and this was happening, would you expect me to give up Kyle for Mother's sake?"

"You're not twenty-one. You're still a baby."

"I thought I was supposed to be so mature."

"You're not acting it now," Grams said.

"In any case, it doesn't make that much difference whether I leave home now or in a few years."

"It makes a great deal of difference," Renee said. "You'll ruin your life if you leave now. I'm surprised at you that you don't see that yourself."

The table was now set, though Anne couldn't remember having done it. "Where's Dodie?" she asked, needing to find someone on whom she could vent her anger.

"Upstairs," Grams said, and added, "When your mother hears about this, it'll make her sick."

"Then don't tell her," Anne said as she walked out of the

room. It was going to be a long siege from now until Kyle was ready to go. Dodie had really set her up for a battering.

"How could you tell them when I begged you not to?" Anne demanded as she burst into her bedroom.

"I told you I would."

"What are you doing?" The room was strewn with clothes and Dodie's suitcases were open.

"You said I had to leave if I told."

Anne bit her lower lip. Angry as she was at her friend, she didn't want to lose her. "Where can you go?"

"Oh, I've had plenty of offers. I only came here because of you. Actually, I had to give up a whole lot of stuff to come."

"I didn't realize what a sacrifice you were making for me," Anne said.

"Yeah, well, it doesn't matter. I'm leaving my address in case Larry or my mother writes. Please forward my mail, okay?"

She wanted to say, "Dodie, you don't have to go," but she kept quiet. Dodie had betrayed her. Yet somehow Dodie had her feeling guilty, as if *she* had let Dodie down. It didn't help to think that it couldn't have been too much fun for Dodie to play second fiddle to Kyle, be dragged along to those aimless parties where no one knew her, and be left to her own devices other evenings when Kyle and Anne wanted to be alone. Not to mention the misery Dodie must have suffered from her crush on Kyle.

"I'm sorry it worked out this way," Anne said.

"You know something, Anne? You're sorry a lot. Being sorry doesn't improve a thing," Dodie said.

"I need to know exactly when we're leaving," Anne said to Kyle when they were alone in his hospital room.

"What for?"

"So I can pace myself. So I know how long I have to outlast them."

"When's Thanksgiving? Make it the day before Thanksgiving."

"The day before? That's cruel," Anne said.

"You want to have Thanksgiving with your family and get carved up with the turkey?"

"Kyle, I have to ask you something."

"Come here and stop looking so miserable, babes. Come lay your head on my shoulder and ask away."

"Would you marry me?" she asked.

"When?"

"Soon. When we get to Arizona, say."

"Your grandmother say you're a bad girl?"

"She doesn't think you love me enough to marry me."

"I wasn't planning on getting married just yet, but I do love you. Okay, yeah. If that'll make it easier for you. We'll do it," Kyle said.

"You better think about it."

"Listen, Anne. Being married's no big deal nowadays. Divorces come fast and cheap. But if the license is important to your family, we'll send them a copy."

It upset her to hear him discount what she valued, but she was too confused to protest. She didn't really want to be married, much less to be divorced when she wasn't out of high school yet.

Each day the family chipped away at her resistance with variations of the same arguments. A few days after Dodie had gone, Lily came into Anne's bedroom. "I want to talk to you, my darling."

"I'm here, Mother."

"For how long? . . . Anne, I know something about infatuation too."

"Your situation and mine aren't the same. You were *married* when you fell for the guy next door. I'm not. I'm free to love Kyle, and he's free to love me."

"But what you're doing is just as foolish as what I did. Do you realize what happens to a woman who has no career training? Look at me. The only kind of job I can get is so low paid I can't even support us both. I have to depend on child support from my ex-husband and help from my mother and sister. How do you think that makes me feel?"

Anne couldn't answer her. Lily had never laid bare her defeat before.

"At least get an education before you throw yourself away on the wrong kind of man," Lily said. "Then you have a foundation to build a new life on if he leaves you."

"Kyle won't leave me. He needs me, Mother."

Lily put her hands over her eyes. When she looked up, she cried, "Anne, don't go. You're all I have."

The naked plea shook Anne as no other appeal had. She burst into tears, but even as she sobbed, she thought that Lily had made her own choices without regard to whom they hurt. Shouldn't her daughter have the same chance? It wouldn't be the end of the world for Lily. Anne would write and call and be back to visit. As for school, she would return to that as soon as she could. Aloud she said, "Mother, I love him so much."

"They getting to you?" Kyle asked her sympathetically when he saw her face.

"They're trying hard."

"You're a lot tougher than I thought you were."

"You know what the other word for tough is, Kyle?"

"What?"

"Selfish. Grams says I'm selfish. She's talking about the same thing you are—just looking at it in a different way."

"I love you, Annie."

"You'd better." She threw her arms around him and rocked his solid body back and forth, thinking of how it would be when they were together every night and could lie in bed and make love until dawn with no one there to stop them.

A week before Thanksgiving, Grams asked for help doing the dish closets where the good dishes were stacked. "They're dirty," she said. "I'm ashamed to have closets like that."

"Oh, Mama," Renee said, "we'll run the dishes through the dishwasher before we use them and wash off the shelves as we take them down."

"There's too much cooking to do everything at once."

"Maybe I'll help you Sunday, Mama," Lily said. "I'm too tired today."

Monday, when Anne came home from school, she heard a funny whimper from the kitchen. Grams was lying on the floor. Beside her lay the stepstool she had been standing on. "I tried doing the dishes myself," Grams said. "You better call your mother or Renee."

"I'll call the doctor first," Anne said. "You may need an ambulance."

The diagnosis in the hospital was a broken leg. The doctor wanted to keep Grams in the hospital a week, but she made such a fuss, they sent her home and arranged to have a nurse with her for the first few days.

"I don't know if they can manage without me," Anne worried, sitting in Kyle's car with the map and a Magic Marker to lay out their cross-country route. "She can't even bathe or dress herself without some help. Renee and Mom share the errands, and I'm doing all the cooking and helping with the cleaning."

"Hey, come on, Anne. If you weren't there, they'd manage, wouldn't they?"

"I don't know how."

"You saying you don't want to come with me?"

"I want to come," she said. "But—could you just wait another three weeks?"

"No way. If you hadn't pinned me down to a date, I'd be gone by now. You think you've got it bad at home? I'm living in poison gas."

"I can't leave this week," she told him. "Maybe you'd better go ahead. I can earn some money meanwhile as a salesgirl after school during the pre-Christmas rush. Then, as soon as the family is back to normal, I'll fly out and join you."

"You will, huh?" He sounded skeptical.

"Yes, I promise. I will."

"Okay. If that's the way you want it."

"Kyle, it's not the way I want it. I can't help what's happened."

"Uh huh. Well, whatever you say." She heard his mistrust.

"Kyle! You still love me, don't you?"

"Yeah," he said. "It's okay. I figured you'd pull something like this."

She tried to convince him she really meant to join him, but he refused to believe her. Still, she could not desert her family now, when they needed her so badly. Three more weeks wasn't so much to ask of him. Letting him go ahead was a risk, but she couldn't live with herself if she left her family in the middle of a crisis.

12

Thanksgiving was a chore. Grams was cranky at her inability to do things herself and wasn't satisfied with what they accomplished under her direction. According to her, the turkey wasn't put in the oven soon enough and the stuffing was dry. Furthermore, their skipping her chestnuts and brussels sprouts specialty because it was too much trouble ruined the festivities altogether.

Lily tried to be cheerful, but Renee was depressed. She always got depressed around holidays, Lily reminded Anne. Those were the times Avery spent with his family and Renee was excluded from his life. Anne could sympathize with Renee. Kyle had gone, driven west with a casual good-bye, as if it didn't matter to him at all that Anne wasn't going with him. She couldn't tell if he was just covering his disappointment or really didn't care.

Missing Kyle was like having a virus that sapped Anne's energy. She had trouble making herself get up and go to school. There she searched out his shape in the halls. Scents made her think of him, and music, those songs of loss and longing that had played over the car radio as they had driven his erratic routes around town. She kept wondering when she would hear from him, if she would hear from him. Suppose she had lost him. The thought made her shiver.

Luckily, she was too busy to spend all her time brooding. A friend of Lily's who was a buyer for the local department store got Anne a part-time sales job at the sweater bar. The work was easy, if not very exciting. Once a customer who knew Anne from school asked what she'd heard from Kyle. "He hasn't written yet," Anne admitted.

"That Kyle!" the girl said cheerfully. "Only he'd take off in the middle of his senior year. He doesn't let anything get to him, does he?"

"Not much," Anne said. She sold the girl a red sweater and watched her leave, depressed by the exchange. The family didn't help her either.

"At least you're getting to bed at a decent hour now that that boy is gone," Grams commented.

"You'll feel better after you start going out with other boys," Lily said. "Would you like to have a party for your friends?"

"I don't have any friends. Kyle and Dodie were my friends."

How could her mother be so understanding of her sister and so insensitive to her own daughter? Anne resented her mother's assumption that Kyle's absence was a minor loss, easy to overcome.

The letter that finally did come from Kyle didn't mention a word about her promise to join him, but she immediately sat down and wrote back:

> It doesn't matter if you don't have a permanent job. I'm coming the day after Christmas. We'll make out O.K.

She even called the airlines so that she could tell him on which flight she was coming. Days passed, a week, but no response from Kyle. She reread his letter, seeking reassurance from the rambling narrative of his adventures. At the first job he had had at a lakeside marina, the boss's daughter had spent too much time fooling around with him. One day Kyle dumped a bucket of water over her. The boss had caught them wrestling and fired Kyle on the spot. Kyle had traded in his car for a motorcycle and found another job at a gas station.

It discouraged her to think that he had had so many new experiences that she hadn't shared. The experiences distanced him more than the miles. Besides, every mention of another female made her jealous. She weighed the single word *love* in his closing. It looked so frail there at the end of his letter.

A Christmas card came from Dodie depicting a funny-looking bird in a Santa Claus suit. Dodie had signed her name, nothing else. That depressed Anne too. Kyle was not the only one she missed.

"Renee, what are you so glum about these days?" Grams asked one evening when she caught Renee looking off into space instead of working on her crossword puzzle.

"Nothing, Mama, just some problems at work."

"You shouldn't let that job bother you so much. You give them enough overtime for nothing as is."

Renee didn't answer. She looked as if she hadn't heard Grams, and Grams frowned at her and glanced at Lily for explanation.

"Tomorrow I'll take you to the doctor to get the walking cast put on, Mama," Lily said to distract her. "My boss said I could take the afternoon off. Maybe I'll go Christmas shopping while you're waiting in his office. I haven't had a chance yet."

"Stay with me in the office. You know I don't like sitting there alone," Grams said.

The walking cast allowed Grams to get around the house better. Renee talked about going to Jamaica on vacation toward the end of January. She wanted her sister to go too, but Lily seemed to find the idea incredible and Grams didn't encourage her. Anne said nothing. She had written a second letter to Kyle asking him to pick her up at the airport in Phoenix, telling him she was definitely coming the day after Christmas.

On Christmas Eve he called.

"Did you get my letter?" Anne asked immediately. Grams was glaring at her from the living room and Renee and Lily were aware that it was Kyle and were listening too.

"Got it. I'll be there," he said.

"And?"

"And what?"

"Are you glad?"

"You know I am, babes. I miss you."

"Good," she said, looking over her shoulder at her family. "Same here."

He chatted on as if the expense of a long-distance phone call were nothing, telling her about the crazy thing that had happened to him on the job, how he had been attacked by a dog who ripped his jacket. The old guy who owned the dog had insisted on giving Kyle money to buy a new jacket, enough so that he could afford a leather one he'd had his eye on. "Wait till you see it, Annie."

"Doesn't he care it's long distance?" Grams hissed.

"That's his business, Mama," Lily said.

Anne was too aware of them listening to pay close attention to what he was saying. She almost said she would see him in a few days, but stopped herself in time. She hadn't told them she was leaving and didn't plan to. She did say, "I love you, Kyle," when he said good-bye. Then she hung up and turned to find their eyes fixed on her.

"What's wrong?" she asked, too happy to believe anything could be now. She wanted to shout with joy at having heard from him, but their grim faces restrained her.

"I thought you'd gotten over him," Renee said.

"Well, I haven't." Impossible family! None of them understood. She dashed upstairs to exult in private and whirled around her room, rolled across her bed, and landed on the floor, where she lay grinning up at the ceiling. He had called after all. Then, after all, he still loved her. She was his girl. She was alive again.

13

"One way or round trip?" the travel agent asked her. She was tensed and ready to lie about her age, but he wasn't questioning her about that at all. She swallowed, willing her quivering stomach to relax. She hesitated.

Looking faintly bored, the young man continued, "Round trip is cheaper and you can always turn in the unused portion of your ticket if you decide not to use it. Of course, then you only get back what you paid over and above the cost of a one-way ticket, which is a lot higher. Get it?"

A round-trip ticket was like an insurance policy, she thought. If it didn't work out, she could come back. But she didn't want to be cautious. That was the part of herself she was leaving behind. "One way will be fine," Anne said.

The night before she was to leave, she went to bed early, wanting a good night's sleep to look her best for Kyle, but sleep wouldn't come. Suppose the taxi arrived too early and she wasn't at the corner where she'd told them to pick her up. Or suppose she got to the corner with her suitcase and Grams came hobbling down the street on her walking cast, wrapped her arms around Anne, and refused to let her go. Grams would hold her until Renee came in high-heeled slippers and Lily in her scuffs to drag her home. Or suppose they caught her as she crept down the stairs with her incriminating suitcase. They would knock her down and lock her in her room to keep her while the plane took off without her. "Selfish, selfish, selfish," Grams would accuse. And Renee would warn, "You'll ruin yourself," and Mother would cry, "You're all I have." Never mind that Anne would be leaving in the afternoon when Renee and Lily were at work. The thoughts skittered through her mind, wild and foolish, wild and foolish as she was going to act, as she had never acted before in her entire little-old-lady childhood.

She tried to conjure up Kyle to calm herself but couldn't. At dawn she thought that it would be easy to turn in the ticket, write Kyle explaining that she couldn't leave her family, who needed her more than he did. Then she could sink back into the security of home. Safe. No galloping heartbeat. Safe and stagnant. Suffocating in the rounds of school and obligations, bakery store surprises to break the monotony, a movie once in a while. Oh, Dodie, she thought, if I were more like you! Dodie would go eagerly, but Anne was weak with fear.

"Are you sick? You look pale." Grams asked her in the morning. Anne had come downstairs late to avoid questions.

"I'm fine, Grams." Guilt weighed her down. In two hours she would be tiptoeing down the steps with her suitcase. The note was already written and left for Mother to find on her pillow.

"Renee keeps after your mother about that Jamaica trip," Grams said, thinking out loud. "Why can't she see that Lily doesn't want to go?"

"It would be good for Mother to go."

"What for?" Grams said. "It's expensive and who's she going to meet?"

"At least it would be something for her to look forward to," Anne said, and when Grams argued that Lily had enough without going so far away for a week's vacation, Anne excused herself and went back up to her room to try and push the immovable minutes past. Reading was safer than getting into a last-minute argument with her grandmother.

Lunch came and Anne forced herself to eat a slice of bread and cheese because Grams was watching. Finally, Grams said she thought she'd lie down for a nap.

"I'll clean up," Anne offered with relief. She did the lunch dishes and left Grams a note on the kitchen table saying *I've gone out.* The vagueness of it would irritate Grams but keep her from getting alarmed before the others got home. Now, get the suitcase, go quietly down the stairs, out the front door. Click of closing. Easy, easier than she had expected. Now for the taxi. Her spirits began to rise. Exciting to be on her way and tonight she would be with Kyle. He would be waiting for her when she got off the plane in just a few hours. Kyle! She did not yet believe it.

The taxi came right on time. She found the airline and queued up, afraid to ask if it was the right line, but it was. Everything was right. She handed over the plaid, soft-sided suitcase that Renee had gotten her for Christmas with college in mind. This was a better use for it, even if Renee wouldn't think so. The ticket stamped, she followed the signs to the gate, got through the baggage check, feverish with anticipation. By the time she was seated on the plane and it had actually lifted off, only a remnant of guilt remained. Instead she felt pride. She had never flown before, but she had done it now all by herself. Competent Anne, cool and no longer cautious. She liked her new, more dashing self, smiled at her faint reflection in the glass. Life was a thrill. Kyle had taught her that. He had kissed her into wakefulness. He had made her live.

No one sat in the seat beside her, and once above the cottony cloud hills and valleys, she saw nothing but blue sky above an endless snowscape. She opened the book she'd brought with her, a Faulkner novel, but couldn't concentrate on the serpentine sentences. She stared out the window, day-dreaming about her life with Kyle. She would make curtains and arrange flowers in hanging baskets, find ways to feed him well on little money. He would be tender and sleep with his arms around her in the night. She would belong to him utterly and he to her.

At Kennedy airport in New York, she sat in the waiting area clutching her book, intent on hearing her boarding announcement: "Rows eleven through fifteen." Her seat was by the window and no one sat next to her. The checkered rooftops of Long Island became a game board below her and then she was riding above the clouds in a pale evening sky.

Just as the steward retrieved the dinner trays, the droning plane began its descent. Below Anne, the ground became a darkness lit with spiderwebs of yellow and green and red lights, a beautiful irregular matrix. She stared entranced as the web became glowing beads of cars streaming down main roads. One light thump and they were down. Jets roaring, the plane rolled smoothly toward the terminal building.

She was nervous again, stomach clutching, heart racing. What would she do if he was not waiting for her? She had no idea of how to reach him. And he was always late. Well, she'd wait. She'd wait all night, and in the morning she'd start calling gas stations. She had some money—enough to buy a few meals so she wouldn't starve. Even enough for a room to stay in, enough for a ticket back home. No, he'd be there. And she was already stronger than she had been. She had flown into a sunset, hadn't she? A sky splotched with red and orange and finally purple in a gorgeous banner on the horizon. She collected her belongings and waited to deplane, trying not to think of how she would feel if he weren't standing there. How was she going to get her suitcase?

In a panic she stalled the exiting line of impatient travelers to ask in a child's strangled voice, "Where do you get your bags?"

"Just follow the signs to the baggage-claim area," the stewardess said.

Anne nodded. A service station. Had he given her the name? She should have brought his letter with her. Maybe he wouldn't be able to take time off. Maybe he worked nights. Maybe he wanted to pick her up, but just couldn't make it. She should have thought of that. But he loved her. He'd be proud that she'd come all this way to him, kept her word, hadn't been such a goody-goody after all.

She walked off the plane through the pale tunnel, through the glass doors into the terminal building. There, behind the railings, stood a crowd of people waiting to greet the travelers. And there, taller than the rest, the big grin on his handsome face just as she had imagined it would be, was Kyle.

She ran, almost knocking over a slow-moving woman, and threw herself into his arms. "Oh, Kyle, you're here!" she cried.

"Didn't you expect me?"

"I was afraid you wouldn't be able to make it, but you're here and I'm here and Merry Christmas." She kissed him and he hugged her.

"You're some Christmas present, babes. I missed you a whole bunch."

"You really did?"

"Really. I really, really did. Hey, are you too tired to go out tonight?"

She had been tired, but now she answered, "I'm fine, just bursting with energy."

"Good, because I've got plans for us. See, usually I work nights and I'm off days, so I never get a chance to hit the night spots, and there's this singer who's supposed to be excellent. She hasn't been discovered yet, so we can afford the tab. Sound good to you?"

She was puzzled. "A singer? But, Kyle, we haven't seen each other since— Can't we go to your place and be alone tonight?"

"Well, my place—I'm crowded in, sort of, so I set you up with a friend. It's only temporary, till I get my act together, Anne. See, this girl Lulu—she owes me a favor. I fixed her van for free, and— She's a good kid. You'll like her."

He sounded so nervous. What was he selling her? "I won't be staying with you at all?" she asked.

"Well, once I get some money together. See, my job doesn't pay all that well."

"I'm going to get a job, Kyle."

"Yeah, well, until then, or until I get something better— Look, it's just as well, isn't it? I mean, what would Grams say if she thought we were shacking up together right away?"

"Grams isn't here. Neither is Renee or my mother."

"Good thing too." He smiled, jollying her along. She didn't like it. Something was wrong.

"We gotta get your bag," he said, and set off.

She clutched his arm as she hurried to keep pace with him and reported breathlessly, "I called your mother the way you asked me to. She said she was glad you were all right. They got the elk's horns and said thank you."

"Yeah. They haven't written. I guess it wasn't such a great present, but I couldn't think of what to get. My father still not letting anyone mention my name in the house?"

"I don't know."

"My mom sent me money for Christmas. I guess she figured I needed it. I would rather of gotten a present. I don't know. The twins sent me a deck of cards with sexy-looking ladies on the back. They didn't write. I guess they don't know what to say."

"You sound a little homesick," she said.

"Not me."

"We'll go back for a visit as soon as we can, huh?"

"First I got to get something going, something worth telling them about. I left as a bum. I don't want to go back that way. . . . How about your family? Anything new?"

"Renee's planning a trip to Jamaica in January and trying to talk Mother into going with her. Grams is getting around better."

"What'd they say about your coming?" he asked.

"Nothing. I just left a note." She shook off the guilt and changed the subject. "Tell me about your job."

"It's a pretty crummy job. I work every night except Sunday, just pumping gas and keeping the station open, not too much repair work involved. Maybe you can come keep me company evenings. You can help pump gas or I can set you up as the cashier."

"Sounds like fun. I missed you so much, Kyle." She squeezed his arm, feeling more confident that it would be all right.

Kyle pulled her bag from the moving line of deplaned luggage and they headed into the darkness of the parking lot.

"I got you a helmet for my cycle," Kyle said. "Borrowed it." He handed her a white plastic bowl while he strapped her bag onto the back of the motorcycle. She looked at the machine apprehensively. Yet another challenge to face. Then she strapped the helmet on and seated herself behind him, thankful that she hadn't worn a skirt to travel in. She hung on tight, shutting her eyes, glad he couldn't see how frightened she was. The cycle made more noise than the plane's jet engines. It felt like a live animal under her. Every time she opened her eyes, she saw highway, standard American highway at night, lined with fast-food places, lit storefronts, and bars with big neon signs. If this was Phoenix, it wasn't pretty. She began to ache with weariness long before he pulled into the back parking lot of a low, square building with a painted sign identifying it as The Black Sheep Club.

"Won't they ask me for an ID?" Anne asked.

"You look older than your age. Act insulted if anyone asks you and say you're twenty-four. Twenty-one sounds like you're lying, but twenty-four is outrageous enough so they might believe you. You don't have to drink anything alcoholic anyway. In this place you can sit around all evening over a couple of beers and a Coke."

She nodded, unstrapped the helmet, and asked, "When will we be alone, just the two of us?"

"Hey," he said. "We're going to have fun tonight, babes. Just be patient, huh?" He brought her close against him and gave her a long, leisurely kiss. "I'm glad you came. I've got a lot to tell you. It's like I've been gone a year. Did I write you I was a bouncer in a bar for a few nights?"

"No, you didn't. Was it hard?"

"Only when the guys I had to bounce were bigger than me. I would've kept the job, but I won too much at the all-night poker games after hours, so the help got a little hostile. That's why I had to trade the old car in. They sort of busted it up one night when I wasn't looking."

"How awful!"

"Well, I had some friends on my side. It pays to have friends. 'Course, they take time to develop. You gotta help somebody move or stick up for them in an argument—"

"Or fix their van."

"Yeah. You'll like Lulu. She looks a little spaced, but she's a really solid dame, takes good care of her two little kids and puts up with her mother too."

"No husband?"

"No. Lulu's not the type for husbands—too independent. Hey, come on. We're gonna miss this singer. She goes on right about now."

It was too dark inside to see anything but the bar that took up most of the right side of the room. Spots lit up the racks of glasses hanging over the bar so they glittered like chandeliers. Kyle led Anne to where a few tables were set up in front of a low stage with a couple of track lights trained on it. Only two of the barrel tables flanked by spindly chairs were occupied. Most of the people in the room were sitting at the bar where Kyle went to place their drink orders. Anne was glad it was dark. She felt too young to be in this place, uncomfortable about the men eyeing her. And yet what did she expect? Being with Kyle always meant having to deal with unrelated experiences. Time was his junk closet. Relax, she told herself. You're with him now.

A girl in jeans with long blond hair and a loose man's shirt over her ample hips wandered onto the stage carrying a guitar. The girl adjusted the mike, smiled briefly at her tiny audience, said hello, and retreated into herself as she plucked her guitar strings. Kyle returned with a paper plate full of popcorn and sat down.

"Coke all right? He didn't have any other soft drink."

"Fine. She looks interesting. Is she the one you want to hear?"

"Yeah." He looked pleased. "She's supposed to be a professor of psychology or something."

"Are you glad you left home, Kyle?"

"Only thing I could have done. Wait until you see the desert, Annie. It's really something out there. And can you believe this weather? Doesn't it amaze you? What's it back home? Below freezing I'll bet."

"Not that bad. It's a mild winter so far. It's nice not to need a winter jacket, though." She laughed to herself. This wasn't the kind of conversation she'd imagined between them, but they had time to say everything now. She touched his hand. He folded his fingers over hers and held on while they listened to the singer, whose voice was sweet and high. She sang about traveling, moving on, longing and looking for something just around the bend or over the next mountain. Kyle seemed deeply moved. Anne felt the loneliness, but it wasn't hers. She wasn't a dissatisfied person always moving on. All she wanted was Kyle and she had him now.

"Isn't she great?" Kyle asked, clapping enthusiastically.

"Yes, I like her voice."

"Hi, Kyle. Is this the 'friend' you said you had to pick up at the airport?"

Anne turned to see who belonged to the husky voice. She saw a curvaceous woman with sulky eyes in a heart-shaped face, a striking-looking woman somewhere in her twenties, Anne guessed.

"Hi, Heller. This is Anne, from Schenectady, New York. Anne, meet my boss, Ms. Heller Adams."

Anne caught her breath. "How do you do?" she said finally despite the woman's unsmiling appraisal.

"I didn't expect to see you here, Heller," Kyle said.

"I didn't expect to be here. Thought I'd have to cover for you tonight, but then my brother, Joe, filled in for me. Aren't you going to ask me to sit down, Kyle?"

"Sure. You're not with anyone?"

"My sister-in-law. She met a feller she used to know. She'll find me when she's ready."

"What are you drinking?"

"A Coors would be fine." She smiled at Kyle and looked at Anne. "It's a long way to come, all the way from New York. You planning on staying long?"

"I'm hoping to find a job."

"That so? What do you do?"

"I'm . . ." She looked at Kyle for direction. He was looking the other way, trying to catch the attention of the bartender. "I'm just finishing high school. I've done retail sales some."

"Thought he might be lonely without you, is that it?"

"I was lonely without him."

"Oh." Heller laughed shortly. "High school. Jail bait, huh. Kyle, you got a high school sweetheart you didn't tell me about. How come?"

"Are we going to listen or not?" Kyle asked, gesturing toward the blond-haired performer who was sing-talking about doing something special on a slow Sunday afternoon. "You heard her before, Heller?" Kyle asked.

"Sure. I come in here a lot. That's where you met me first, remember? At the bar."

"Oh, yeah."

"Took him home and gave him a job and a place to stay the first night I met him. That's how all my mistakes happen—too impulsive. That's me."

"You got any complaints about the way I run the station for you, Heller?" Kyle demanded, tight-lipped.

"No. You're honest. That's one good thing. But any moron can run a station nights. It's not that hard, is it? Lots of guys can do *that* for me." She stood up abruptly. Her beer hadn't been delivered yet. "Your bed will be waiting for you when you're ready for it, Kyle," she said distinctly, and nodded at Anne. "Hope you enjoy your stay, honey." She walked off slowly, as if she couldn't care less what she had left behind.

Anne stared at nothing, unable to look at Kyle. The singer was into another number, but Anne didn't hear a word of it. Any doubt she might have about Kyle's relationship to his "boss" had been eliminated by the tone of the woman's voice. "Your bed will be waiting for you." Anne's eyes went to Kyle's fingers, which were tearing a matchbook to pieces. He was listening to the singer with a frown that meant he wasn't hearing either.

"Would you like another Coke?" Kyle asked.

"That woman—" Anne said.

"What about her?"

"What is she to you—besides your boss?"

"I think she made that pretty plain. I shouldn't have risked taking you here. I thought she'd be at work. She said she had to cover for me." He looked at Anne earnestly. "Listen. I know you're just a kid, but see if you're grown up enough to understand this much. There's love and there's sex. The two don't always happen at the same time. With you and me, what's special is—"

"No wonder you never got around to writing me," she said.

"I wrote you."

"Once."

"You want to pick a fight now?" he asked.

"It never would occur to me to look at another guy, much less— And I like sex as much as you do."

"Anne, what I have going with Heller is strictly a convenient arrangement. It has nothing to do with love. I *love* you."

"Then we don't mean the same thing by the word," she said.

"So we don't. What's that got to do with anything? Look, let's not fight here. You're tired. After a good night's sleep, you'll feel better and we'll talk about it. Okay? Let's get out of here."

Kyle laid some money on the table and took her arm. He even remembered to pick up her suitcase, which he had checked with the bartender. Then they roared out of the lot as if they were being chased and pulled into traffic in front of an outraged driver, who followed them for a mile blasting them with his horn. Anne buried her head against Kyle's back, squeezed her eyes shut, and grasped him in fear, wishing she had hands free to cover her ears. They rode forever.

When he finally stopped, she was grateful. No more noise. No more wind swiping at her or bone-shaking vibrations to endure.

"This is Lulu's place," he said.

She saw a doll-sized ranch house, dittoed along a curving drive by what looked like dozens of other identical houses, each a different color. Lulu's house had a gaudy ceramic Mexican—mostly hat—pulling a wagon on the space that would have been a front lawn if there had been any. In the bar Anne had felt caught in a surreal world. This was more of the same. She couldn't believe it when she saw him knocking on the front door. After what had happened, was he just going to dump her at the house of a stranger like a homeless pet?

The girl who opened the door wore a man's pajama top and had her hair up in curlers. Kyle beckoned Anne closer and introduced her. "The kids just went to sleep," Lulu said. "We got to be quiet or they'll be all over the place again. Hi, Anne."

"Hi, Lulu," Anne said with automatic politeness, "I'm sorry to be putting you out like this."

"Oh, no bother. I'll just leave you some sheets on the couch and you can make the bed up yourself. I'll leave a towel too, in case you want to wash up. Hope you don't mind if I just roll back in bed. I'm beat. I'm waitressing, and I'm not used to being on my feet."

"You go back to bed, Lulu," Kyle said. "I'll just say good night to my girl here and take off."

"Fine. Listen, Anne, my mother comes in to watch the kids in the morning. So if you see a strange lady, that's her." Lulu smiled a wan smile and padded back into the house, leaving the door ajar.

Kyle looked at Anne. "Would you rather go to a motel?"

"No." She didn't want to walk into a stranger's shadowy living room alone, but she didn't want to go to a motel either.

"You still mad at me?" he asked.

"Not mad. Just disappointed."

"Yeah, that's me, 'disappointing.' I disappoint myself sometimes too. It was bad luck you came out right now. In a month it might've been better. I don't know, Annie—I still love you."

"Do you?"

His hands touched her shoulders lightly, as if to make sure she was really there. "You're my girl. You're the special one in my life. Only when you're not around there's all that empty space. It doesn't mean anything how I fill it. You're the only one means anything." He folded her against him surely and his lips came down seeking hers. She shivered and backed out of his arms.

"Just a couple of hours ago you wanted me. What's changed?" he asked.

"Please, Kyle."

"You really are a kid, you know? You still think like the dragon lady taught you. You're going to have to grow up, babes, and start accepting life like it is."

"I don't think so," she said.

"All right. I'll call you in the morning." He left her abruptly, angry with her again. She waited until he had walked the motorcycle down a few houses, kicked it into life, and roared away. She was left with the open door, a watching moon, and the strangeness. Inside, the living room smelled faintly of urine and sour milk. Lulu had opened the couch for her. Open, it filled most of the room. The couch, an armchair, a TV, and various wheeled toys were all the furnishings. Anne switched on a lamp and gingerly made the bed up with the sheets that were tossed on top of it. The door to the bathroom was open. She got her toothbrush out of her suitcase and brushed her teeth, trying to make it all seem normal. In the mirror her eyes looked as weary as Lulu's.

Anne lay on the sleep couch in the dark and listened to her heart beating, slowly, as if it wanted to stop. Tears kept leaking out until eventually she fell asleep.

She woke up early, knowing without question what she was going to do. Lulu had already left. The mother, a heavyset woman who looked at Anne suspiciously, was in the kitchen getting the children's breakfast. Anne made up the sleep couch and went into the bathroom to change her clothes. Then she introduced herself to the woman, who asked if she'd like a cup of coffee, but with such grudging politeness that Anne said, "Thank you, no. I'd just like to call the airport, if I may use the phone."

"That's a local call. That's all right."

The children, who looked about two and five years old, stared at her solemnly while they ate. The telephone directory had to be retrieved from under the little girl.

Just as Anne was looking for the airline's telephone number, the phone rang. The older child, a boy, answered it. "It's for you," he said, and offered her the receiver.

"Anne? You're up early," Kyle said. "I'll be over in a little while. What do you say we take a drive into the desert today? There's a spot I want to show you. We've got till five when I'm due at work."

"I'd rather you just drove me back to the airport, Kyle. I'm taking the next flight home."

"Why?"

"I can't talk about it now." Not with a kitchen full of strangers listening.

"Hold everything. I'll be right over."

She thanked the woman and took her suitcase outside to wait for Kyle. She was perched on the suitcase, still waiting, when the children trotted out with their grandmother behind them. She locked the door and herded the kids into a car. Then she nodded at Anne. The kids waved good-bye and Anne waved back. No exchange of words. It struck her as funny. If Kyle didn't pick her up, what would she do?

She looked anxiously at the houses evenly spaced along the curved, flat street on either side of her. A huge cactus, fifteen feet high with holes in its side, stood in the yard across the way, dwarfing the house behind it. To Anne's amazement, a bird poked its head out of one of the holes, looked around, and retreated. Gravelly-looking sand covered the ground. Except for varying shapes of cacti, nothing green seemed to grow. One house had artificial grass in its yard, so green it hurt the eyes. She could have been on an alien planet, she thought, especially since the only sign of human life was the sound of cars swishing by on the highway. No children played around these houses; no one walked in the street. The only moving thing she saw was a small lizard, the size of her middle finger. It crept down from the brim of the ceramic Mexican hat, reached the knees of the sleeping figure, and climbed down its leg to the ground.

She had been sitting there for hours. At least, it seemed like hours, but she had no way of telling the time because she hadn't wound her watch before going to bed. She would go to the house with the fake lawn and ask if she might use their phone to call for a taxi to take her to the airport. But suppose the taxi cost so much that she couldn't buy a ticket home! She had been a fool to reject the safety net of a round-trip ticket. She shivered, although the morning was already so hot she felt uncomfortable in her jacket and took it off. She would have to knock on the stranger's door. As for the taxi, she could ask how much it cost before she ordered one. If worse came to worse, she'd have to try to hitch. Was he punishing her by not coming? Making her understand how much she needed him? If so, it wasn't working. The longer he stayed away, the more she wanted to get away, go home where the ground was winter-deadened and the trees were leafless and she was truly loved.

By the time Kyle's motorcycle charged to a stop in front of her, Anne was crying bitterly. "Hey, babes!" he called. "Look up. I got something to dry those tears." He had the long narrow box from the florist strapped on his back. He disentangled himself from the motorcycle and from the odd backpack and handed it to her, arms out, a peace offering.

She shook her head at him. "You're so late."

"Had to stop and get you these. I tried to get long-stemmed red, but the lady said yellow were fancier, so yellow you got."

Reluctantly she opened the box and stared at the expensive,

crisp golden heads nestled with frills of delicate ferns in the crinkly green paper.

"I only got eight because that was all I had on me. Read the card." He looked so happy, his handsome face glowing with confidence.

She read the card. *To my one and only. Love, Kyle.* But she wasn't his one and only. Sorrowfully, she sniffed the roses, holding the box like a baby in her arms. They had no smell. What did he expect her to do with eight long-stemmed yellow roses when she didn't have any water or anything to put them in?

"You wasted your money, Kyle," she said.

"You won't forgive me?"

"How can I? There's Heller."

"I told Heller you're my girl."

"So?" she asked.

"So she understands now."

"What does that mean? Are you going to move out of her house?"

"Well, sure, when I can," he said. "Right now, though, she happens to be my boss as well as my landlady, and if we want to eat— Come on, babes. Be reasonable. It'll all work out."

She looked at him in amazement. Didn't he respect her at all? "Don't waste these," she said, handing him the box with the flowers still in it. "Give them to Heller or Lulu or somebody. And take me to the airport, please."

"Anne, what's the matter with you? Don't start acting like a spoiled brat. For God's sake, you can't expect me to be faithful to you when we're half a country apart and who knows when we'll make it together again. Look at it from my point of view, huh?"

"No," she said. "I don't need to do that. I put you first. I proved that. Now I have to consider where to put myself."

"You want me to take you to the airport?" he said coldly. "Okay, have it your way, but you're gonna be sorry. You're messing up our relationship for nothing." He tossed the box of flowers away, hoisted her suitcase onto the back of his bike, lashed it in place, and said grimly, "Get on."

She looked at the flowers already wilting in their pristine box on the walk where he had flung them. The waste made her cry. Crying, she climbed on behind him, strapped on the helmet, and clasped him around the waist as he took off. She had cried herself out by the time he let her off at the arrivals area of her airline.

"Do you have enough money to get home?" he asked, not looking at her.

"Yes."

"I'll leave you here then."

"Fine," she said.

His jaw worked as if he had things to say, but he didn't say them. He gave her one hurt, angry glance and took off. She picked up her suitcase and walked wearily into the terminal and over to the ticket counter.

Her plane would take off in two hours.

In the waiting area at the gate, Anne sat thinking. However she tried to fit the fragments of the past twenty-four hours together, they made no sense—the singer in the nightclub, the bed in the stranger's living room, the insinuating voice of Kyle's female boss. It had been a grotesque sideshow. What had happened to his values? She squeezed her eyes shut against the answer, which she already knew. Nothing had changed about Kyle. He was no different than he had ever been. He'd chosen her, and she had let her pride in that disguise him in her eyes. Kyle's girl! Who was she then if she wasn't his anymore? Lily's daughter, Renee's niece, Grams's child?

Anxiously, she searched for a self that was purely Anne and couldn't find one. Was she only defined by her relationships to others? Wasn't there any core to her? Kyle's girl! It disturbed her to think how willing she had been to limit herself to that. It had always pleased her to be called mature. Foolish, she saw now, to have been flattered. Mature meant fully developed and she wasn't. She was a person in the process of becoming. In that lay her promise.

14

She had been away only one day, but it seemed weeks had passed between her leaving and returning. Snow was falling at the Albany airport, quarter-size flakes scattering from a profligate sky, small stars on a dark afternoon.

"Here it comes," the airport taxi driver said. "Did ya hear the report? We're in for a big one. Bet we get six inches at least. Kind of late for a white Christmas, though."

"Not too late," Anne said quietly. She had taken the first seat behind the driver. Four middle-aged men with attaché cases in hand got in before the driver slammed the doors shut and started off. She listened to the solemn thumping of her heart. How would they greet her? With tears and anger. Too late now to regret what she must have done to them. Grams was right to call her selfish.

By the time the taxi dropped her off in front of her house, a papering of white covered the surfaces of street and bush and house and car. She paid her fare with her last five-dollar bill, picked up her plaid suitcase, and stood facing the house. All its angular features were hidden behind the scraggly trees. How dear the homely house looked now. Her home, where she belonged. The door opened as if Grams had been watching for her and Grams stood there with her hands out, framed in the yellow light of the hall lamp. "Anne!"

"Grams, I'm so sorry," she cried, running up the walk to fling herself on her grandmother and hug her.

"Thank God you're back. Are you all right?"

"I'm fine."

"Nothing happened to you?"

"Nothing bad."

"Call your mother right away. She went to work, but she didn't sleep all night. None of us did. Renee's chewing her fingernails again, and she hasn't done that since she was a child."

"Will you forgive me, Grams?"

"So long as you're back, that's all that matters. Thank God nothing happened to you!" She touched Anne's cheek with a pathetic gratitude and no accusation in her eyes.

"Grams, I love you," Anne said, meaning it at that moment. While her grandmother sniffed back tears and wiped her eyes, Anne dialed the number of the dress shop.

Anita, the shop owner, answered and said Mrs. Busca was busy with a customer and would call back. "She doesn't have to," Anne said. "Please just tell her her daughter's home and will see her at dinner."

"You're home!" the haughty Anita screeched. "Lily, Lily, your daughter's back!"

A second later Lily's voice called Anne's name. "Yes, Mom. It's me."

"Oh, my baby!" Lily sobbed.

Anita got on again. "I'm sending your mother home to you,

but don't you ever do a thing like that again, young lady. You don't know the grief you caused."

"No . . . yes . . . I won't," Anne said. "Thank you."

Next, Grams made her call Renee. Renee answered in her authoritative business voice, which went mellow as soon as she heard Anne speak. "Anne, darling, you're all right?"

"I'm fine."

"What happened, then? Why did you come back so soon?"

"It didn't work out."

"Did he give you a bad time?"

"It's all right, Renee. All I got was disillusioned."

"If that's all, you're lucky. You'll get over him and next time you'll know better. I hope. Listen, we have to celebrate. I'll stop at Alfred's and bring home a whipped-cream cake."

"Oh, Renee! First you yell at me, and now you're going to make me a party?"

"Well, it's true you don't deserve one, but so what. Tonight we'll indulge ourselves."

Anne was helping Grams get dinner ready. "All I have is pork chops," Grams complained.

"Pork chops are fine, Grams."

She wondered when Grams would start telling her how rotten she had been. Soon enough probably, but all Grams said was, "Your mother thought you'd be all right. She said you were too sensible to get in any real trouble. I don't know. At your age I'd never have dared to run off like that. I was still going along with what my family did. We visited relatives and went for rides in the country for fun. I didn't start seeing boys until I was eighteen years old."

"I know, Grams."

"Well, times have changed. Not for the better, either, as far as I can see."

"In some ways it's for the better. Girls have more chances today."

"To do what? To get in trouble?"

"To make something of themselves, Grams."

Grams grunted in disgust. "Look at your aunt and your mother," she said. "Renee made something of herself, but she's never had the husband and children she wanted, and she's not a happy person. Your mother got the husband and children and what does she have left? Only you."

"So what is that supposed to teach me?"

"To do better."

"I'll try, Grams." For once Anne could see through the nagging to the love behind it. She put down the carrot she was peeling and gave her grandmother a kiss. Tomorrow, no doubt, they would be at odds again, but today she could feel sustenance in the bond between them. It was true, Anne thought. Grams did want good lives for each of them. Their failures were her heartaches, and her nagging was part of her caring.

A while later Lily burst into the kitchen. After hugging Anne and weeping a little, Lily picked up the dress box she'd dropped on a chair. "Welcome home, my angel girl." She thrust the box at Anne.

"A present? Why give me a present? You ought to be giving me a hard time for what I did to you."

"You nearly killed us all with worry, but that's past. Open the box."

Anne lifted the coral velvet dress out of its wrappings. "It's beautiful, but I don't have anyplace to wear it."

"You will. I saw it on the sale rack and couldn't resist buying it for you. Try it on."

Anne slipped out of her skirt and sweater and into the dress right there in the kitchen.

"It's a perfect fit," Grams said. "Looks as if it were made for her."

"Doesn't she look like a dream in it?" Lily exclaimed fondly.

Anne ran upstairs to see herself in her mother's full-length mirror. It was hard to see through the tears that kept flushing her eyes. They loved her so much. She had been willful and blind and made them miserable, and they were still glad to have her home. She dried her eyes and checked the mirror again. Was there a hint of character in the wide-eyed girl staring back at her? She was smiling at herself when the doorbell rang. Still smiling, she ran downstairs to open the door for Renee.

"The prodigal returns!" Renee said. "You look gorgeous in that dress. I see your mother upstaged me. Well, she's your mother after all. Here, put the cake in the refrigerator." Renee began brushing the snow off her coat.

As they sat finishing dinner at the kitchen table, watching Lily serve up generous slices of the whipped-cream cake, Anne said, "I ought to run away more often."

"Don't you dare. None of us can take another night like last night," Renee said.

"Do you want to tell us what happened, Anne?" Lily asked.

Anne shrugged, embarrassed to reveal how Kyle had let her down. She summarized quickly, "I thought I was the only girl in the world for him, but when I got there I found out he was living with a woman. She owns a gas station. She's his boss."

"Didn't take him long to adjust, did it?" Renee asked.

"He's not ready for a one-girl relationship, and I'm not up for any other kind."

"I should say not!" Grams said.

"I thought I was special in his eyes."

"You are special," Lily said.

"Especially foolish to fall for a boy like him," Renee said.

"Do you still love him?" Lily asked.

Anne considered. "I shouldn't, but he's really— There's a lot to love in Kyle."

"But you're not 'in love' anymore," Lily said.

"He was never for you," Grams announced.

"Next time pay attention when we tell you somebody's no good," Renee said.

"Renee, we've all made mistakes," Lily said.

Renee answered contritely, "All right, I know. Don't listen to me. I'm all raw nerve endings." And that, Anne knew, was her fault.

Six days of vacation remained to Anne. She was alone in the house with Grams most of the time, and there wasn't much to do besides read and do housework. Anne took long walks in the snow, making fresh tracks where she could along with fresh resolutions. She would be a better person, more thoughtful, more generous. She would reach out to others and make friends. She would develop new interests and participate more. Instead of telling her family she was sorry all the time, she would give them reason to be proud.

The hardest task she set herself was to write to Dodie. Anne missed her and wanted her back. Still, she thought Dodie had acted badly. The letter took hours to compose, and Anne wasn't too hopeful of getting a response even after she mailed it. She had written:

> Dear Dodie,
>
> I care about you very much. I lost more than you

did when I sent you away, but the truth is, I feel you shouldn't have interfered. I was already pushed around by too many people close to me, and I couldn't take another person trying to direct my life just then. But I shouldn't have been so all or nothing about it. Instead of telling you to leave, I should have just had it out with you. So I was wrong, and I hope you can forgive me and be my sister-friend again.

Love, Anne.

She put the letter out of her mind the way she might buy a raffle ticket and not think about winning a prize. She read and cleaned out her bedroom closet and painted it, a job she'd put off for years. She baked cookies and even played gin rummy with Grams one afternoon. Evenings she went shopping with her mother for clothes for Lily's Jamaican vacation. She had finally agreed to go with Renee, and the two sisters were giddy in anticipation of their trip.

When Anne thought about Kyle, the old feelings came back and she missed him. Then she had to remind herself that Kyle was just a dream she had had. For her own sake she had to learn to live with reality. To be alone again. Well, she could survive being alone. She remembered Christmas vacations when she'd spent hours playing board games with her little brother or helping him build a snow fort. She'd taken him sled riding—so many things done for his sake that she herself had enjoyed. She missed Chip more than ever now.

Friday afternoon Grams called, "Pick up the telephone, Anne. My hands are greasy."

"Anne, it's Dodie."

"Dodie!"

"Who else? Prepare yourself. You are going to the best New Year's Eve party you've ever been to."

"That won't be hard. I've only been to one," Anne said. "It was last year. Kyle took me. I didn't know a soul and it was terrible." It was Dodie! It was Dodie! Anne could barely stand sounding cool when she was so excited.

"Well, you won't know a soul at mine either," Dodie said. "But you'll like lots of people and I'll introduce you around, and if you don't find anybody you like enough, you can just stick with me. Wait till you see what I'm going to wear! It's the best costume I've ever had. Larry sent it to me from San Francisco. It's an embroidered kimono. I look gorgeous in it. What have you got to wear?"

Anne thought of the coral velvet. "Well, I have a dress, but —Dodie, I can't come to your party. I don't have any money for traveling. I spent it all going to Kyle."

"Oh? How did that go?"

"I came back the next day."

"It figures," Dodie said. "Wanna tell me about it now or wait until you get here?"

"I just told you. I don't have any money."

"Right. Well, you ask Renee or your mother to lay it out. It'll be my Christmas gift to you. But make it cheap. Come by bus or train."

"Oh, Dodie!" Anne burst into tears.

"What's the matter?"

"You know. You're too much."

"Never mind that. I'm even more than you think. I went on an eating binge when I got home and put back all the weight I took off at your house. Right now I'm on a starvation diet, and I need help. Could you leave tomorrow? That way we'll have the weekend together. You can help with the party and hold me back every time I edge toward the refrigerator."

"I'll ask," Anne said. "I'll call you back tonight after dinner, okay?"

"But you will come?"

"Yes, I'll come. . . . Dodie?"

"What?"

"You really are my friend again?"

"Don't be stupid. I never stopped. Some ties aren't so easy to break, you know," Dodie said.

Anne gripped the receiver, so choked with tears she couldn't speak.

"Anne, are you there?"

Grams appeared at the kitchen door and said anxiously, "That's a long-distance call, isn't it? Why are you still on the phone?"

Dutifully, Anne said good-bye and hung up. Then she began to laugh through the spilling tears. Some things never changed and some ties were binding, and it was so funny that she could be happy to end up with what she'd had at the beginning. Except that she no longer feared her family might keep her forever. When the right time came, she knew now she had the strength to open the door again and go.